2nd Edition

Personal Budget Kit

www.enodare.com

Bibliographic Data

- International Standard Book Number (ISBN): 978-1906144982

- Printed in the United States of America

- First Printing: August 2013

- Second Edition: March 2017

Published by: Enodare Limited
                                                Athlone
                                                Co. Westmeath
                                                Ireland

Printed and distributed by: International Publishers Marketing
                                                22841 Quicksilver Drive
                                                Dulles, VA 20166
                                                United States of America

For more information, e-mail books@enodare.com.

Warning and Disclaimer

Although precautions have been taken in the preparation of this kit, neither the publisher nor the author assumes any responsibility for errors or omissions. No warranty of fitness is implied. The information is provided on an "as is" basis. The author and the publisher shall have neither liability nor responsibility to any person or entity with respect to any loss or damages (whether arising by negligence or otherwise) arising from the use of or reliance on the information contained in this kit or from the use of the forms, documents or spreadsheets accompanying it.

IMPORTANT NOTE

This kit is meant as a general guide to preparing a personal budget. While considerable effort has been made to make this kit as complete and accurate as possible, everyone's personal situation is different. As such, you are advised to update the information within this kit with your own personal research and, where necessary, take financial advice before acting on any information contained in this kit.

The purpose of this kit is to educate and entertain. It is not meant to provide financial advice or indeed any other advice. The authors and publisher shall have neither liability (whether in negligence or otherwise) nor responsibility to any person or entity with respect to any loss or damage caused or alleged to be caused directly or indirectly by the information or forms contained or referred to in this kit or the use of that information or those forms.

ABOUT ENODARE

Enodare, the international self-help publisher, was founded in 2000 by a group which included lawyers, entrepreneurs, business professionals, authors and academics. Our aim was simple - to provide access to quality business and legal products and information at affordable prices.

Enodare's Will Writer software was first published in that year and, following its adaptation to cater for the legal systems of over 30 countries worldwide, quickly drew in excess of 40,000 visitors per month to our website. From this humble start, Enodare has quickly grown to become a leading international self-help publisher with legal and business titles in the United States, Canada, the United Kingdom, Australia and Ireland.

Our publications provide customers with the confidence and knowledge to help them deal with everyday issues such as setting up a company, running a business, preparing a tenancy agreement, making a last will and testament and much more.

By providing customers with much needed information and forms, we enable them to protect both themselves and their families through the use of easy to read legal documents and forward planning techniques.

The Future....

We are always seeking to expand and improve the products and services we offer. However, in order to do this, we need to hear from interested authors and to receive feedback from our customers.

If something isn't clear to you in our publications, please let us know and we'll try to make it clearer in the next edition. If you can't find the answer you want and have a suggestion for an addition to our range, we'll happily look at that too.

USING SELF-HELP KITS

Before using a self-help kit, you need to carefully consider the advantages and disadvantages of doing so – particularly where the subject matter is of a legal, financial or tax related nature.

In writing our self-help kits, we try to provide readers with an overview of a specific topic, as well as some sample documents that can be used to assist readers in achieving their financial or legal objectives. While this overview is often general in nature, it provides a good starting point for those wishing to carry out a more detailed review of a topic.

However, we cannot cover every conceivable eventuality that might affect our readers. Within the intended scope of this kit, we can only cover the principal areas in a given topic, and even where we cover these areas, we can still only do so to a moderate extent. To do otherwise would result in the writing of a text book which would be capable of use by financial professionals. This is not what we do.

We try to present useful information and documents that can be used by an average reader with little or no financial knowledge. However, it may be the case that your personal circumstances are such that a review by a financial advisor might be much more appropriate in the circumstances. For example, where your debts are in arrears or where your credit rating has been severely damaged. In such cases, personal reviews can be more beneficial.

It goes without saying (we hope) that if you are in any doubt as to whether the documents or suggestions in this kit are suitable for use in your particular circumstances, you should contact a suitably qualified professional for advice before using them. Remember the decision to use these documents or to act on any information in this kit is yours! We are not advising you in any respect.

Anyway, assuming that all of the above is acceptable to you, let's move on to exploring the topic at hand.........personal budgets.

TABLE OF CONTENTS

AN INTRODUCTION TO PERSONAL BUDGETING

Do you know how much money you actually receive on a daily, weekly or monthly basis? More importantly, do you know where it all goes? Most people can venture a guess, but many would be surprised to discover how far from reality that estimate actually is. In today's electronic payment culture, the use of debit cards, visa cards, standing orders, direct debits, money transfers and countless other money transfer methods makes it increasingly difficult to keep up with the flow of money. It is for this reason that personal budgeting has become so much more important even for people of more moderate means.

Personal budgeting seeks to bridge the gap between guessing and knowing. By using a budget to carefully analyze how you receive and spend money, you can gain an amazing insight into your financial life and, more importantly, how to live within your means. By understanding and prioritizing personal cash flow, we can see "the big financial picture" and make better financial decisions. We can set realistic goals and put an organized, results-oriented budget plan in action to achieve them. We can take complete control over our finances.

For many, budgeting can feel like a long-term punishment involving sacrifice and abstinence. However, when done right, the opposite can be true. By paying closer attention to our incomes and expenses, we learn to understand that creating and living within a budget is essential to managing the finances that underscore every aspect of our lives. By budgeting, we don't have to fear an unexpected medical or repair bill, because we've planned for that contingency. We don't run out of money when the bills are coming due, because we're keenly aware of how much we need to set aside and when. We create savings plans for the things we need and want in life. In the same way that a blueprint maps out a plan for building a home, a budget maps out a plan for achieving financial security.

Without a clear picture of your finances, it's difficult to know whether your goals are compatible with your current lifestyle, or what new goals you could strive for simply by altering your existing lifestyle and spending habits. By creating a budget, you establish a livable plan to reach your goals—whether that means saving for a big-ticket item such as your first home or just having the financial security of knowing you can ride out a tough economy.

Money, like time, should never be wasted. Making a promise to do better in the future—after the holidays or the summer vacation, for example—is merely delaying the invaluable opportunity to gain control of your present and future.

Now is the ideal time to commit to making and sticking to a budget. And it's not hard to do. A budget finds balance between the money that comes in and the funds that go out. In between, there is the decision-making process. Do I need that new car? Can I really afford that concert ticket? How much should I be saving each month to achieve my goals and how can I create a plan that I can stick to?

In this kit, we'll guide you step-by-step through the process of creating and living with a personal budget. We'll show you how to set goals, both short and long-term. You'll learn how to gain control of your personal cash flow. You'll discover when you need to make adjustments to your budget and how to do it wisely. Most of all, this kit will show you that budgeting isn't simply about adding limitations to your living but rather the foundation for living better by maximizing the resources you have.

Budgeting can be fun when you realize the rewards that it will deliver. Look at the gains—the healthy savings account, the ability to pay for unexpected expenses, and the security of your financial future. But there's more to it than simply monetary benefits. By being in control of your finances, you'll also reduce the stress and worry in your life and with that control often comes increased self-confidence too! You might even find yourself sleeping much sounder!

It all starts here, by committing to being the guardian of your money and your future. No one else is going to do it for you, so empower yourself, take charge and let's budget!

CHAPTER 1

WHY YOU NEED TO BUDGET

Chapter Overview

In this chapter, we look at the advantages of creating and adhering to a personal budget. We cover the different types of budgets you can make and the various items that need to be considered when creating a personal budget.

Why Budget?

Every day, we are inundated with thousands of offers and opportunities to buy goods and services. Some of these offers are direct while many others are so subtle we may never even realize it. Take an average day, for example. You get up in the morning and make your way to the bathroom. You use a shampoo that recommends the use of a specific type or brand of conditioner to get the best possible results from the shampoo. You use a face wash that suggests the use a particular skin exfoliation product or face mask to help improve the results. You dress yourself in your designer suit or clothes, go to the breakfast table and pick up a box of cereal. On the back of the box, a simple suggestion that you add blueberries, strawberries, and other fruits – to help improve your dietary intake. You pick up the morning paper, there's a sale on at your local jeweler and you've had your eye on a particular watch for months now. As you glance over the top of the paper at the TV, you see that Oprah has a guest on her morning show recommending the latest New York Times best seller – a must have for all self-help enthusiasts. You make your way to the train station and purchase a ticket. On the back are discount vouchers for your local hair salon and restaurant. As you exit the train, you see advertisements all round including cheap vacations to Egypt….and heaven knows you could do with a break. You land at the desk and turn on your computer. You have mail! The local tailor is offering a special 2 for 1 on work shirts and, as a loyal customer, you have been offered first dibs! As you finish reading, you receive a text from your phone company who has aligned itself with a national gym chain offering you a reduced membership opportunity…although you have to sign up for twelve months. That's not a problem because you'll use the gym – right? The day continues…..and everywhere advertisements hit you, everywhere opportunity presents itself. Everywhere, you are forced to receive and evaluate offers from manufacturers, suppliers and distributors. In fact, just like the average person, you see up to 3,000 advertisements each day!

With all these offers and opportunities, and of course all the easy ways in which we can purchase or subscribe to them, it should come as no surprise to learn that our spending naturally increases over time. This increase often brings with it financial difficulty including an increased dependency on credit cards, overdrafts and other short-term financing facilities. With so many reasons to dispose of our hard-earned wages, and so many ways to do it, it's critical to create a support system to manage our finances. That's what a personal budget will do.

By creating a plan that forecasts earnings and expenses, we can get our financial lives under control so that when opportunities to spend money arise we clearly know whether or not it makes financial sense to take advantage of them. A budget enables us to make decisions with confidence, to plan ahead, and to build a cushion of savings even when it appears virtually impossible to do so.

Creating a Personal Budget

Taking the time to review your finances and create a budget is a valuable investment that will reap ample rewards, both in the short and long-term. In preparing any budget, there are a number of steps which should be followed. Each of these steps is summarized briefly below.

1. Understand your financial situation

   Creating a budget requires a close look at how we live our lives. The analysis gives us an in-depth view of our income weighed against our expenses, which in turn allows us to determine whether we are living within our means. We can see where the money flows in and out, including how much and how often. In so doing, we gain an invaluable perspective on what we're doing well and where we can make changes. Without a budget, we're playing a dangerous guessing game and risk overspending and the financial troubles that come with it.

2. Set goals

   We all have wishes and many of them require setting aside money—whether for buying a big ticket item that you have long desired or just creating a savings cushion. By creating a detailed plan, we can convert those wishes into goals, with measurable steps that hold us accountable and guide us toward ultimate achievement.

3. Identify cost savings opportunities

   From eating on the go to paying bills without reviewing them, we overlook many chances to reduce spending and increase savings. A budget requires a close review of all expenses and can motivate our thinking as we begin to see ways to make better use of our money.

4. Create a savings plan

   It might seem impossible to set aside money but a budget can provide a gateway to savings. Even if you're living paycheck to paycheck, the budgeting process can provide valuable insights into ways in which you can find even a few dollars a week to build towards a savings goal. In fact, many people who have already committed to saving ten percent of their paycheck say that they readily adjust to living a bit leaner, and that the knowledge of a growing savings account is a steady reward.

Establishing a budget is the first step toward achieving financial freedom. Postponing this essential step is delaying your attainment of a secure future.

Budgeting in 3 Easy Steps

Every budget comprises of three main steps:

1. Find out where your money is going.

2. Identify where you can make savings and cut-backs.

3. Keep track of your spending and stick to your savings and cut-back plan!

The Rewards of Sticking to a Budget

There are many reasons to create a budget, but if you don't adhere to it, the effort is wasted. Living with a budget will provide a powerful return on the investment of time as, day by day and week by week, you get closer to achieving your ultimate goals.

Consider these stress-reducing benefits that will come from sticking to your budget plan:

1. Reduce or eliminate debt

   Whether loans or credit card balances, debt is a heavy burden. If living debt-free is one of your goals, you can create a budget that will allow you to focus on that task. Watching the balances shrink away each month will provide constant motivation to stick with your budget.

2. Build savings

   As you find ways to set aside money by budgeting carefully, you accrue savings that can be invested in a manner that will deliver the return you need. You can start small and build an investment portfolio or simply keep your money in an interest bearing savings account. As you stay within your budget or discover new ways to save more money, you give yourself the gift of greater financial security.

3. Control expenses

   Creating a budget provides a clear picture of where you spend money. Living within that budget enables you to make educated financial decisions. You learn to differentiate those expenses that are worthwhile from those that will cause you to detour from the agreed plan. The added knowledge will continue to reward you with the ability to stay on course and avoid spending more than you can afford. Overspending means that you often borrow money (e.g., use credit cards), which incurs interest charges and fees that create another expense—and a wholly avoidable one.

4. Improve credit ratings and scores

Good credit is essential to making major purchases, like buying a car or home. The better your credit rating, the better your interest rate on loans and credit cards. Working within a budget will ensure that bills are paid on time and debt is reduced—both of which are key factors in building a strong credit score.

5. Seeing progress

A budget isn't simply a document that jump-starts a financial management plan and ceases to apply. It needs to be updated and followed continuously. You should regularly review your budget and compare it to your actual income and expenses to ensure you're staying on track. Seeing the progress towards building savings, reducing debt, and staying within the limits of the budget plan shows that your efforts are working. This will give you the gratification that is key to ensuring that you remain true to the established plan.

When preparing a budget, commit to sticking with it right from the outset. A budget will only deliver results when it is followed consistently. Straying from the approved financial plan will only prolong achieving those important goals that prompted you to create your budget in the first place. Remind yourself of those motivators when you're tempted to overstep the boundaries of the budget.

 Important Tip

Before creating a budget, you should create a list of (i) the reasons why you want to control your finances, especially the negative experiences that you're currently having and (ii) all the benefits that you will achieve by sticking to your plan.

Types of Budgets

There are two basic methods for personal budgeting. Each one will help to track income and expenses, so you just need to determine which approach best suits your style.

Envelope Method

Make a separate envelope for each regular expense, such as rent or mortgage, car payment, taxes, utilities, groceries, and savings. Determine how much money from each paycheck will be necessary to cover each bill. Then put that amount in the envelopes on every payday, before spending any money on other items. This way the required funds will be available when needed. This method is often useful for those who receive their wages in cash rather than directly into their bank accounts.

Spreadsheet Method

Create a spreadsheet that maps out all income and expenses by week, month and/or year. Start with your monthly income sources at the top and underneath insert a line item for each required monthly expense. Subtract those expenses from your income to determine your monthly disposable income. That amount will then be budgeted for savings and other financial goals.

The most important factor in choosing the best budgeting method for you is to determine which approach will be the most effective and easy to use for you. If spreadsheets overwhelm you, consider the envelope method. Or create a hybrid approach that makes it easy to track expenses and measure progress. Use the budget spreadsheet that comes with this kit or look for budgeting software programs and smart phone apps that appeal to you and your particular needs. Be sure to include the necessary categories and sub-categories to provide an accurate perspective on your income and expenses.

In this kit, we will be focusing on the spreadsheet method. As such, and in order to complete the exercises throughout the ensuing chapters, you should download a copy of the budget spreadsheet that accompanies this kit. Download instructions for the budget spreadsheet are contained on the next page.

Key Requirements for a Successful Budget

Before moving on to the next chapter – *Analyzing and Tracking Your Current Finances* – it's worth identifying some of the factors that will have the greatest impact on ensuring your success in creating and sticking to your budget plan. These are set out below.

1. Be as accurate as possible

   Don't make guesses about your income and expenses. Look at recent paystubs to determine your gross pay and each amount that is withheld from it (including taxes and any voluntary contributions such as health insurance or union fees). For expenses, review bank statements, credit card statements, bills, till receipts and other past payments to see how you actually spent your money.

2. Tailor the budget categories to your needs

   For budgets to be accurate, the spreadsheets on which they are prepared need to be structured so that they contain sufficient scope to allow you precisely monitor your spending habits. The budget worksheets and spreadsheets that come with this kit contain pre-set categories into which you can

ENODARE'S BUDGET SPREADSHEET AND WORKSHEETS

To download your budget spreadsheet or the worksheets contained within this kit, simply visit the link specified below. You will be required to create an account and enter the unlock code presented below. Once completed, you will then be able to download all documents associated with this kit.

You should save your budget spreadsheet and worksheets in a location on your computer that will be easy to access (such as your desktop) during the course of preparing and monitoring your budget.

Web Address: http://www.enodare.com/downloadarea/

Unlock Code: BUD20173

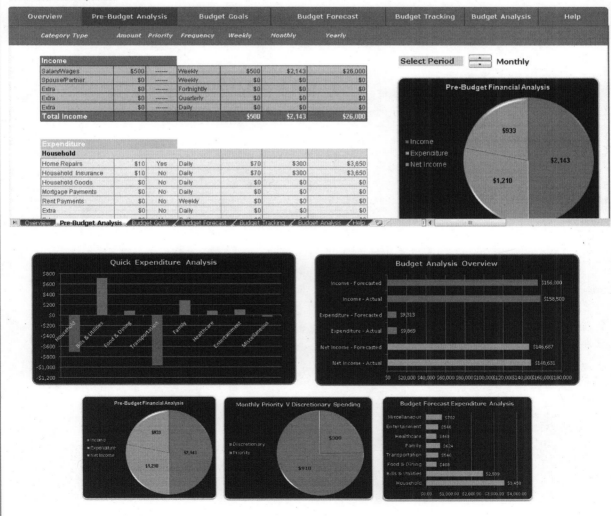

enter your own information, without starting from a blank page.

For example, under the "Pre-Budget Analysis" tab of the budget spreadsheet, you will find a category for transportation expenses. This category, in turn, is sub-divided into rows for gas/fuel, car insurance, car repairs and more. While a general template like this can be very useful as a starting point, in order to ensure that your budget is all encompassing you will need to add customized headings and categories as needed. For example, if you have one child in college and another in high school, you might want to separate school supplies and expenses for each child rather than group everything under one general expense. This will give you a lot more visibility over your spending habits.

3. Track cash expenditures

The money spent for a coffee, magazine, newspaper, taxi ride, tips, parking, lunch, or a short stop at the grocery store or pharmacy can add up quickly and not be recorded with your other expenses. Keep receipts or jot down the cost for every purchase and include them in your weekly and monthly accounting. We'll show you how to do this in the next chapter.

4. Keep a positive attitude

Budgeting is a positive step towards a secure financial position. It shouldn't be painful or punishing. Remember the goals for creating the budget (and read them regularly to keep you motivated) and focus on the benefits of staying on task.

Introducing the Budget Spreadsheet

The personal budget spreadsheet that comes with this kit allows you to easily add details of your current incomes and expenses. Once these details are added, you can use the budget spreadsheet to help create future spending goals and, more importantly, to help you monitor how successful your budgeting efforts are by mapping your budget goals against your actual spending.

The budget spreadsheet contains a number of tabs. A brief introduction to each of those tabs is set out below.

Overview

The "Overview" worksheet provides you with an overview of what the budget spreadsheet does and how to use it. It explains each of the individual worksheets, how information should be entered into those worksheets, what those worksheets show and how the information in those worksheets interacts with other worksheets.

Pre-Budget Analysis

The "Pre-Budget Analysis" worksheet is perhaps one of the most important worksheets in the spreadsheet. In this worksheet, you will enter details of your pre-budget monthly income and expenditure. You will need to do this before you start the budgeting process.

In the worksheet, your expenses will be broken down into different categories such as "household", "family", "transportation", etc. These expenses will be further broken down by frequency of spending such as daily, weekly, monthly, etc. These breakdowns will allow you to closely analyze your spending. That analysis will be aided by a number of graphs and charts which will quickly illustrate where your money is being spent (on a weekly, monthly and yearly basis), whether or not that money is being spent on discretionary or non-discretionary (priority or non-priority) items and whether you generate a 'profit' or 'loss' for each particular financial period.

Budget Goals

This worksheet (which is optional to complete) allows you to set monthly spending goals by reference to your average pre-budget monthly spending habits. Details of your average pre-budget monthly expenses are automatically pulled in from the "Pre-Budget Analysis" worksheet. Once this information is pulled in, you will then need to add details of your desired monthly spending goals for each of the different expenses listed. The worksheet will then automatically calculate the level of savings that you would make for each specific expense - both on a dollar basis and on a percentage basis - by achieving your goals. The worksheet will also calculate the total savings that you would make if you achieved all your monthly goals.

For example, if you spend $900 per month on entertainment pre-budget and wish to reduce this to say $600, you will simply need to insert $600 in the "Goal" column opposite the details of your pre-budget monthly spending level for entertainment. The worksheet will then calculate the monthly savings that you would make by achieving that monthly goal (i.e. $300) and the percentage reduction you would make to your entertainment expenses (i.e. 33.33%).

On the right hand side of the worksheet, there are a number of graphs which provide you with graphical summaries of your pre-budget spending compared to your spending goals.

Budget Forecast

Having determined your pre-budget monthly spending and set some goals for monthly savings, the next thing that you may wish to do is to create an actual budget to help you achieve those goals. This can be for any period up to twelve months and can even include your partner's income and expenses in addition to your own.

By making a budget, you will have clear view of your projected income and expenditure level over a defined period of time if you meet your monthly budget targets. While there may be an element of guess work in preparing a budget, it can still be very beneficial for getting a longer term view of your finances.

As you will see, the top section of the worksheet contains a cash flow analysis which quickly gives a summary of your projected income and expenditure on a monthly basis. The information in this section will be generated from the information that you enter in the blue (income) and green (expenditure) sections immediately below it. In these blue and green sections, you will need to enter details of your projected or budgeted income and expenditure for each month. Of course, if you only want to complete details for a few months rather than an entire year, that's perfectly fine.

The right hand side of the worksheet contains graphical analyses of projected monthly and annual cash flows. Using the up and down arrows immediately above the graph, you can change the graph so that you can view a specific month or the entire year as a whole.

Budget Tracking

Now that you have set some monthly goals and prepared a budget to help you achieve those goals, it's time to start recording your actual monthly income and expenditure for each month of your budget in order to determine whether or not they are falling in line with the budget you have created in the "Budget Forecast" worksheet.

The top section of this worksheet contains a cash flow analysis which quickly gives a summary of your actual income and expenditure on a monthly basis, as well as details of the net income (i.e. the 'profit' or 'loss') for each month. Underneath that, there is an indicator for each month which tells you whether your budget for the year to date is "On Track" or "Over Budget". If you want to see whether your budget is on track for a specific month or category of expense, instead of the year to date, you will need to view the "Budget Analysis" worksheet.

Budget Analysis

This worksheet provides a more detailed comparison between the monthly income and expenditure targets that you set in the "Budget Forecast" worksheet and your actual income and expenditure for those same months as set out in the "Budget Tracking" worksheet. The graphs on the right hand side of the worksheet give you a clear picture of how these compare on an expense by expense basis, thereby allowing you to quickly identify the areas in which you are currently overspending - whether it is "entertainment", "food & dining", "transportation" or otherwise.

Help

The budget spreadsheet uses Microsoft Excel to enable you to quickly and easily create and plan your budget. From time to time modifications of the worksheets may be required. Listed in this section are tutorial links which will enable you to modify the spreadsheet as required. Here you will find help on formatting worksheets, creating and using formulas for calculations and much more. Should you need additional help and support, our customer service team are always available at support@enodare.com.

CHAPTER 2

ANAYZING AND TRACKING YOUR CURRENT FINANCES

Chapter Overview

In this chapter, we'll move into the budget development stage. The first step will be to start collecting the information necessary to accurately calculate your income and expenses. It's only by having this information that you can accurately determine where you can make savings and cuts in order to reach your financial goals.

Getting Started

Now that you have an idea of the importance of budgeting, the next stage is to analyze your finances and your financial position generally. This analysis will involve a consideration of what income you have, what debt you owe, the expenses that you need to meet and those that you simply incur. It is only once you have an understanding of these amounts that you can set realistic goals for your finances and prepare a budget that will allow you to meet those goals.

The importance of obtaining accurate information in relation to your finances cannot be overstressed. Without this information and the related figures, your budget will not accurately reflect your financial circumstances and will be doomed to fail right from the outset. Diligence and honesty are key requirements to making your budgeting exercise worthwhile.

6 Steps to Preparing a Personal Budget

1. Make a list of all of your expenditures – daily, weekly, monthly and yearly.

2. Make a list of your incomes.

3. Decide on key expenditures and prioritize the more important expenses.

4. Identify where you can reduce costs and/or increase your income.

5. Enter all of your financial details and goals on to the budget spreadsheet included with this kit.

6. Review the first draft of your budget and make any necessary adjustments.

You should start the process by gathering all or as much of the documentation listed below as you can:-

- Bank statements, credit card statements, loan statements, mortgage statements and any other relevant statements.

- A statement of your gross and net income, such as your monthly or weekly pay slips.

- Statements of any other sources of income – such as rental income receipts or dividend receipts.

- Copies of household and personal utility bills such as phone, gas, electric, etc.

- Copies of all monthly bills such as healthcare expenses, membership subscriptions, etc.

- Receipts – remember it's the little things that will count later.

In each case, you should obtain details for the last 6 to 12 months where possible. From these documents, we will begin to paint a picture of your personal financial situation. The figures in these documents will be used to create your budget later on in the preparation process.

Exercise 1 - Getting Prepared

In order to get ready to prepare your budget you will need the following documents and items:

• Weekly Expense Tracking Worksheet

• Monthly Expense Tracking Worksheet

• Monthly Expense Forecasting Worksheet

• Yearly Expenses Forecasting Worksheet

• The documents listed in the "Getting Started" section above

• Notepad

• Calculator

• Pencil and eraser

You can download your weekly, monthly and yearly expense worksheets from **enodare.com** **See page 17 for more details.**

Calculating Your Total Income

Your income provides the means by which you can achieve your short-term and long-term financial goals. For many people, this income is the amount of their paycheck, after all the deductions have been taken out. However, there might be other cash streams that bring money into the household accounts, including:

- Alimony or child support

- Bonuses

- Commissions

- Child welfare

- Income from rental properties

- Investment interest and dividends

- Pension or retirement income

- Proceeds of sale of personal items

- Stock dividends

- Spousal support

- Social security benefits

- Social welfare benefits

- Unemployment benefits

Be sure to gather details of all your revenue sources so as to have a proper accounting of your financial position. Start by making a note of your weekly income. Include any payments that you receive every week, on a regular basis. Then list those other income sources and identify when those payments are received (e.g., weekly, monthly, quarterly, annually). Once you have all of your details to hand, you will need to enter them in the top section of the "Pre-Budget Analysis" tab of the budget worksheet.

 Important Tip

It is wise to only include income that you will definitely receive in your budget. The reality is that work bonuses, tax refunds or cash gifts from relatives are subject to situational changes particularly in the current economic climate. As such, you may find yourself in financial trouble if you spend money in the hope that these additional incomes will be received and you never actually receive them.

Total income may vary from week to week and month to month, depending on your situation. Some people who are paid hourly will have fluctuations in their income. Others who earn occasional bonuses or commissions will also have to plan more carefully to ensure the budget figures are accurate.

When forecasting income, use your best estimate based on past experiences. If you know that a certain payment you receive is going to increase (e.g., a raise or bonus), be sure to enter the increased amount during the month when the change takes effect, and not before.

Don't guess figures. Refer to pay stubs and statements to get actual figures for all revenue sources. Remember that you're better to err by under-estimating income than by over-estimating. If you inflate your income, you will find yourself having to cut costs later in order to make up the difference in your budget.

Exercise 2 - Calculating Your Income

If you have not already done so, you will need to download the budget spreadsheet that accompanies this kit. This spreadsheet can be downloaded from enodare.com. See page 17 of this kit for details.

The spreadsheet contains a number of specific tabs, each of which works to help you assess your current financial position and to prepare and monitor your budget. If you are not comfortable using spreadsheets, you can download the Income Worksheet that accompanies this kit. This worksheet is similar to the spreadsheets, except that you will have to print it off and fill it in by hand and, of course, there are no automatic calculations carried out.

Using the spreadsheet, select the "Pre-Budget Analysis" tab and insert details of your income into the blue section at the top of that screen. You will need to enter details of the source of your income, the amount of that income and the frequency in which you receive it. You can select the frequency by clicking the drop down arrow that appears in the "Frequency" cell. Once you have included all of your details, save your changes and move on to the next section.

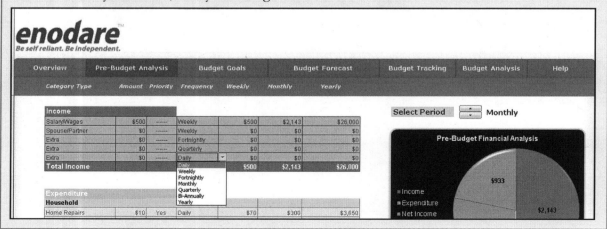

Calculating, Tracking and Forecasting Your Expenses

Once you have determined your income levels, the next step in the budget planning process is to find out where your money goes after you receive it. You'll do this by carrying out a detailed analysis of your expenses over a period of time. This analysis will help you:

(i)   identify your expenses;

(ii)   quantify and categorize those expenses;

(iii)   identify the frequency of those expenses i.e. whether they are daily, weekly, monthly, annual or once-off expenses; and

(iv)   use information about your expenses and spending patterns to calculate and forecast your future spending habits.

By having a clear understanding of how you spend your money over the course of a week, a month or even a year, you will be better able to formulate a budget that will be reflective of the actual financial life you live.

Identifying your expenses can be done in a number of ways. Perhaps the most straightforward of these ways is to review each of the financial documents we mentioned at the start of this chapter - such as your bank statements, credit card statements, etc. The information contained in these documents should give you a fair indication of how you are spending your money and on what. It will also give you much of the information needed to complete the worksheets that we'll be using later on in this chapter. For example, if your credit card statements show that you spend $20 a week on gasoline, you will be able to put an appropriate figure into your budget spreadsheet for that expense or, if you are using the worksheets, into each of your weekly, monthly and yearly expense worksheets as appropriate.

Similarly, if you have any old receipts lying around you'll be able to use them to help identify some of the items that you may have bought for cash. Cash items will often include daily purchases such as coffees, public transport and similar costs. You will be able to use the information appearing on these receipts in much the same way as your credit card and bank statements to help you complete your budget spreadsheet and/or expense worksheets.

Of course, while the use of old financial statements and receipts can give you a very good picture of your spending habits, it doesn't give you a complete picture. The only way to get this complete picture is by actively tracking and/or forecasting your spending habits over a particular period of time. The information gained from these tracking and forecasting exercises will give you an incredibly accurate picture of your spending habits by taking into account everything from your daily cup of coffee in Starbucks to your monthly purchase of "My Home" magazine, and more.

Expense Tracking and Forecasting Exercises

The worksheets included with this kit allow you to track and forecast your expenses in two particular ways. You can either:

(a)   track your expenses for a full week and use the details collected over that week long period to forecast your likely monthly and/or annual expenses ("Weekly Method"); or

(b)   track your expenses for a full month and use the details collected over that period to forecast your spending over the course of a year ("Monthly Method").

Needless to say, tracking your expenses for a full month will allow you to forecast your annual expenses a lot more accurately than you could using only your weekly expense figures.

If you wish to use the Weekly Method, you will need to start by completing the Weekly Expense Tracking Worksheet and then completing the Monthly Expense Forecasting Worksheet. If you wish, you can then complete the Annual Expense Forecasting Worksheet to get a longer term forecast. Alternatively, if you plan on using the Monthly Method, you will start by completing the Monthly Expense Tracking Worksheet and then, if you wish, the Annual Expense Forecasting Worksheet.

Weekly Expense Tracking

In order to track your expenses over the course of a week, you will need to keep careful records of what you spend your money on during each of the seven days in that week (the "Trial Week"). You can keep these records in a number of different ways. For example, you could keep these records using:-

(i)   one of the many financial apps that are available for download via your smart phone;

(ii)   a pocket notebook; or

(iii)   a copy of the Weekly Expense Tracking Worksheet that comes with this kit.

Weekly Expense Tracking Worksheet

While you are free to choose any of the above tracking methods, we recommend the use of the Weekly Expense Tracking Worksheet as it has been specifically formatted to help you gather the information that you require for preparing your monthly and annual expense forecasts, as well as your budget. For example, it contains specific columns for each day of the week as well as additional columns for monthly, annual and other periodic expenses. To help you keep track of the different types of expenses that you incur, each column is also divided into a number of sections reflecting many of the most common expense types such as entertainment, household, travel, etc. Of course, if you have a unique expense category that isn't included in the worksheet, you can always add any new sub-headings or categories that you like!

Whatever method you chose to use to keep track of your expenses, you will need to bring your 'record keeper' around with you for the entirety of the Trial Week. If you purchase something during this Trial Week, just make a note of that item in your record keeper. Your note should include details of the item purchased, its cost and its frequency of payment. If you make a payment that is not a normal weekly payment but is in fact a monthly, annual or other periodical payment, you should make specific note of that as, for the purposes of calculating your weekly spending, these items will be noted but ignored. If you accidently include annual or monthly purchase in your weekly purchase figures, it will result in skewed monthly and annual expense forecasts.

Important Tip

Remember also to keep track of any payments you make using your debit and credit cards during the trial week.

You should also consider bringing an envelope with you in which to tuck receipts, rather than stuff them in a pocket, wallet or handbag where they might be accidentally discarded or destroyed.

In making your purchases during this Trial Week, it's important that you don't alter your spending habits in any way. If you do, you will not get a clear picture of where your money goes on a daily and weekly basis and, as a result, your entire monthly/annual expense forecasts as well as your budget will be distorted. For example, if you skip your $2.95 morning coffee from Starbucks during the Trial Week, and therefore don't include it as an expense in your records, it could appear that you have an extra $1,076.75 in annual disposable income to avail of than you actually have.

Once you have completed this exercise and noted all of your payments over the Trial Week, you should have clear details of your spending habits broken down by category and frequency of payment. At this stage, for organisational reasons, if you haven't used the Weekly Expense Tracking Worksheet we suggest that you transfer details of all your expenses to that worksheet. You can then add up the totals for the week and transfer your figures as appropriate to your Monthly Expense Forecasting Worksheet and, if you wish, to your Annual Expense Forecasting Worksheet.

While many budgeting publications suggest that you transfer the full set of balances from one worksheet to another, it is not recommended that you do so without some careful review. This is because there could be items in your Weekly Expense Tracking Worksheet that, for example, are in fact monthly, semi-annual or even annual expenses. As such, if you transfer the balances directly without careful consideration and review, you could end up accidentally including an annual expense four times in your Monthly Expense Forecasting Worksheet! This would give you a 'fairly' skewed view of your normal spending patterns. This is why it's important that you review your Weekly Expense Tracking Worksheet carefully so that you clearly distinguish between your weekly expenses and other periodical expenses; and that you only transfer normal week to week expenses to the weekly columns in the Monthly Expense Forecasting Worksheet. If the expense in question is incurred on a monthly or annual basis, then it will need to be transferred to the appropriate column in the Monthly Expense Forecasting Worksheet.

Specific information on completing the Weekly Expense Tracking Worksheet and transferring balances is attached to the worksheet itself.

Resource

A copy of the Weekly Expense Tracking Worksheet is set out on page 98 of this kit and can be downloaded from enodare.com (see page 17 for details).

Using the Budget Spreadsheet to Track Expenses

You can use the budget spreadsheet that comes with this kit to track expenses in much the same way as you can using the Weekly Expense Tracking Worksheet. In fact, given its flexibility, the budget spreadsheet can be used to track expenses over any particular period of time.

To add details of expenses to the budget worksheets, simply click on the "Pre-Budget Analysis" tab of the spreadsheet. You will be able to add expenses in this section by simply inserting them directly into the spreadsheet. However, in adding details, be sure to select the appropriate frequency of expenditure whether it be daily, weekly, monthly, annually, etc. This will ensure that the software takes proper account of those expenses when calculating your weekly, monthly and annual expenses.

After you have entered all of your details, you will be able to view details of your weekly, monthly and yearly expenditures by simply selecting the relevant period using the arrows located immediately above the "Pre-Budget Financial Analysis" pie chart which appears in the "Pre-Budget Analysis" tab of your spreadsheet.

Prioritizing Expenses

If you are using the budget spreadsheet, then as you enter each expense in the "Pre-Budget Analysis" tab, you should also specify whether that expense is a priority (non-discretionary) expense or not (a discretionary expense). If the expense is a non-discretionary or priority expense, you can indicate this by selecting the "Yes" option from the drop down menu that appears when you select the cell in the "Priority" column. Similarly, if the expense is not a priority expense and is in fact a discretionary expense, you can select "No" from the drop down menu. The selection of whether an expense is a priority expense or not is important as the spreadsheet will display in the "Pre-Budget Analysis" tab the amounts that you are spending on both discretionary and non-discretionary items. This will help you assess where savings can be made at a later stage. We will discuss prioritizing expenses in a little more detail in Chapter 4.

Exercise 3 – Tracking Your Weekly Spending

Print off a copy of the Weekly Expense Tracking Worksheet and enter details of all of your expenditures over the course of a week. Include only those items that you pay for during this week long period. Do not include items that you pay for on a monthly or annual basis by attempting to divide them by 4 or 52 (as the case may be) to get an approximate weekly figure. You need to capture each expense based on its frequency of payment!

Do not make any changes to your spending habits during this week. The sole purpose of this exercise is to identify your normal weekly spending habits. It is only by completing this exercise that you can properly identify the areas where you can make savings and cutbacks so that you can set and achieve realistic budgeting goals.

At the end of the week, if you wish to use the Monthly Expense Forecasting Worksheet you can print off a copy of the worksheet and fill it in manually using the data from the weekly worksheet. This worksheet will supplement the Weekly Expense Tracking Worksheet by giving you a clearer picture of where your money goes on a monthly basis.

Alternatively, if you wish to use the budget spreadsheet, you can transfer all of the details from the Weekly Expense Tracking Worksheet into the "Pre-Budget Analysis" tab of the budget spreadsheet. Remember to carefully input the amount of each expense and select the frequency of payment for each such expense.

A copy of the Weekly Expense Tracking Worksheet is set out on page 98 of this kit and can be downloaded from enodare.com (see page 17 for details).

Monthly Expense Tracking

In order to track your expenses over the course of a month, you will need to keep careful records of what you spend your money on during that period. You can do this in much the same way as outlined above for recording your weekly expenses.

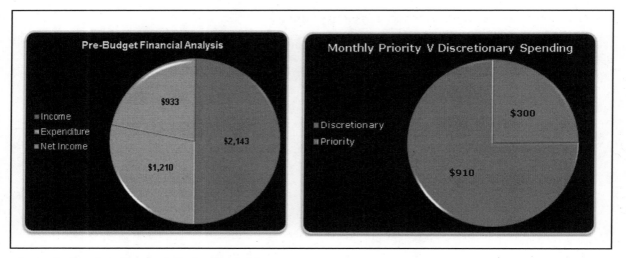

A sample chart from Enodare's Budget Spreadsheet

Monthly Expense Tracking Worksheet

Again, while you are free to use any method for collecting this information that you wish, we strongly suggest that you use the Monthly Expense Tracking Worksheet. Like the Weekly Expense Tracking Worksheet, the Monthly Expense Tracking Worksheet is divided into specific columns, having one column for each day of the month as well as a number of extra columns for other periods. In addition, each column is sub-divided into a number of expense sections which allow you to quickly identify the specific types of expenses you spend your money on and the total of each such expense incurred during the month long trial period.

The Monthly Expense Tracking Worksheet will be completed in much the same way as the Weekly Expense Tracking Worksheet; the only difference is that it will be completed over a period of up to 31 days rather than 7 days. During the month long trial period, you will add details of each of your expenses/payments during that period. Remember; do not change your normal spending habits during that period.

Once you have completed this exercise and noted all of your payments over the course of the month, you should have clear details of your spending habits broken down by category and frequency of payment. If you have not used the Monthly Expense Tracking Worksheet to collect daily information during the month long trial period, you should transfer all of the details you have collected to that worksheet now. Once this worksheet is completed, you should add up the totals for the month so that you have a clear summary of your spending habits over the course of the month long trial period. If you wish to get an indication of how your spending will look over a year long period, you can transfer the balances from the Monthly Expense Tracking Worksheet to the appropriate columns and rows in the Annual Expense Forecasting Worksheet.

Specific information on completing the Monthly Expense Tracking Worksheet and transferring balances is attached to the worksheet itself.

Using the Budget Spreadsheet to Track Expenses

As already alluded to, you can use the budget spreadsheet that accompanies this kit to track expenses in much the same way as you can using the Monthly Expense Tracking Worksheet. Details on how to use the spreadsheet have been set out in the previous section on weekly expense tracking.

Exercise 4 – Tracking Your Monthly Spending

Print off a copy of the Monthly Expense Tracking Worksheet and enter details of all of your expenditures over the course of a month. Include only those items that you pay for during this month long period. Do not include items that you pay for on an annual or other periodic basis by attempting to divide them by 52 (or otherwise) to get an approximate monthly figure. You need to capture each expense based on its frequency of payment!!

Do not make any changes to your spending habits during this month. The sole purpose of this exercise is to identify your monthly spending habits. It is only by completing this exercise that you can properly identify the areas where you can make savings and cutbacks so that you can set and achieve realistic budgeting goals.

At the end of the month, if you wish to use the Annual Expense Forecasting Worksheet you can print off a copy of the worksheet and fill it in manually using the data from the weekly worksheet. This worksheet will supplement the Monthly Expense Tracking Worksheet by giving you a clearer picture of where your money goes on an annual basis.

Alternatively, if you wish to use the budget spreadsheet, you can transfer all of the details from the Monthly Expense Tracking Worksheet into the "Pre-Budget Analysis" tab of the budget spreadsheet. Remember to carefully input the amount of each expense and select the frequency of payment in respect of that expense.

Monthly Expense Forecasting

Once you have completed your Weekly Expense Tracking Worksheet, the next step in understanding your financial spending habits is to prepare a forecast of your general spending habits over the course of a month. This is done by:-

(i)   taking the daily balances in the Weekly Expense Tracking Worksheet and replicating them across a period of 28 days in the Monthly Expense Forecasting Worksheet. This should give you a fair estimate of your day-to-day spending over that period;

(ii)   accounting for the remaining three days of the month (on the assumption that there are 31 days in the month) using suitable figures extracted from your Weekly Expense Tracking Worksheet;

(iii)   transferring any payments listed in the "Monthly" column of the Weekly Expense Tracking Worksheet into the Monthly Expense Forecasting Worksheet; and

(iv)   supplementing those expenses with details of all other expenses that you pay on a monthly basis which have not already been included. These monthly costs can include expenses such as mortgages, rent, car payments, loan payments, credit card payments, utilities (e.g., electricity, phone, heat, water, cable television and internet service), club membership fees (e.g., fitness, yoga, aerobics, gymnastics, dance, etc.), insurance premiums (e.g., health, auto, homeowners, rental, etc.), prescriptions, garden maintenance, house cleaning, trash removal and much more.

If you have paid or are planning to pay an annual, quarterly or once-off expense during the month in respect of which you are preparing your forecast, make sure to add it under the "periodic or annual" column. As previously mentioned, to avoid skewed forecasts, you need to separate all of those expenses which you pay for on a monthly basis from those which are not paid monthly. Otherwise, if you include these non-monthly expenses in the total expenses for that month, you will have a substantially inflated and inaccurate figure for monthly expenses.

Apart from giving you a fairly accurate indication of your monthly expenditures, preparing a monthly expense forecast is important as it will provide you with the basic building blocks upon which you will prepare your monthly budget in the ensuing chapters. While you will amend your expenditure levels in your budget, the budget itself will look remarkably similar to your monthly expenditure details.

If you want to get a picture of your annual spending, you can transfer the balances from your Monthly Expense Forecasting Worksheet to your Annual Expense Forecasting Worksheet. Specific information on completing the Monthly Expense Forecasting Worksheet and transferring the balances to the Annual Expense Forecasting Worksheet is attached to the worksheet itself.

Exercise 5 – Forecasting Your Monthly Spending

Print off a copy of the Monthly Expense Forecasting Worksheet and fill it in using the data you have accumulated in the Weekly Expense Tracking Worksheet. Once you have added this data, you should add details of all the supplemental monthly expenses not already taken into account in the weekly worksheet. Once completed, you will have a clear picture of where your money goes on a monthly basis.

Annual Expense Forecasting

Having completed your Monthly Expense Tracking Worksheet or your Monthly Expense Forecasting Worksheet, you may want to get a glimpse of how your spending might look over the course of a year. To do this, you will need to complete the Annual Expense Forecasting Worksheet. This is done by:

(i)   taking the monthly balance from the Monthly Expense Tracking Worksheet or, as the case may be, the Monthly Expense Forecasting Worksheet and replicating those balances across a period of 12 months in the Annual Expense Forecasting Worksheet. This should give you a fair estimate of your month-to-month spending over that year long period;

(ii)   transferring any payments listed in the "Annual" or "Periodic"columns of the Weekly Expense Tracking Worksheet, the Monthly Expense Forecasting Worksheet or the Monthly Expense Tracking Worksheet;

(iii)   supplementing those expenses with details of all other expenses that you pay on a periodic basis which is greater than one month such as quarterly, semi-annual or annual expenses. These costs can include expenses such as quarterly insurance premiums, property taxes, car repairs and membership fees. If you're self-employed and pay quarterly income taxes, include your estimated tax payment—but only if you haven't accounted for the deduction in your income figures. Think also about those bills that creep up once or twice a year such as annual insurance premiums, tuition fees, automobile registration fees, or possibly one or more balloon payments on a loan; and

(iv)   adding details of any anticipated occasional expenses and non-essential expenses (see below).

Occasional Expenses

A column has been included in the Annual Expense Forecasting Worksheet for occasional expenses. This group will be comprised of essential costs that are not regular, like medical bills, car or home repairs, computer maintenance, pet care (veterinarian, grooming, boarding) and school supplies (including costs for field trips). These payments are usually unforeseen but you should include an approximate figure in your annual expenses forecast to cover these items. You should review your financial records to help determine how much these items cost during the previous year and that cost can be used as an indicative figure in your forecast. Although, be careful not to duplicate the entry if you have already included some of these costs in your weekly or monthly totals. Once determined, the relevant (or estimated) figure should be included in the annual worksheet under the "Occasional Expenses" column or in the spreadsheet if you are using it.

Non-Essential Expenses

Finally, a column has also been included in the Annual Expense Forecasting Worksheet for non-essential expenses. These are those incidentals that mount up because we're not looking closely at them. This list includes clothing, gifts, entertainment (dining out, movies, sporting and event tickets, video games, music downloads), vacations, personal care (hair styling, manicures), hobbies, subscriptions (video service, satellite radio, magazines), and other similar luxuries. A good way to identify some of these expenses is to look at your credit card statements. If any of these expenses have not been taken into account in the spreadsheet or in any of the previous worksheets, you should add them to your spreadsheet or to your Annual Expenses Worksheet under the "Occasional Expenses" column so that they are included. Once done, you should have a clear indication of your total annual expenditure. At this point, it can be daunting to see that the list of expenses is a long one; however, remember that the more extensive your list is at this point, the more comprehensive and effective your budget will be.

Exercise 6 – Forecasting Your Annual Spending Tip

Print off a copy of the Annual Expense Forecasting Worksheet and fill it in using the data you have accumulated in the Monthly Expense Tracking Worksheet or, as the case may me, the Monthly Expense Forecasting Worksheet. Once you have added this data in the manner set out above, you should add all the supplemental annual, occasional and non-essential expenses that are also referred to above. Follow the instructions on the worksheet as directed. Once completed, you will have a clear picture of how you spend your money on an annual basis.

Important Tip

You can view details of your weekly, monthly and yearly expenditures in your budget spreadsheet by simply selecting the relevant period using the arrows located immediately above the "Pre-Budget Financial Analysis" pie chart which appears in the "Pre-Budget Analysis" tab of your spreadsheet.

Understanding Your Expenses

In getting ready to prepare a budget plan, it's not just enough to simply know what expenses you have. You also need to understand the nature and importance of these expenses. You need to know whether they are fixed in price or variable, whether they are recurring or once off, whether they are necessary or not and, where they are necessary or desired, how important each is. In the ensuing sections, we'll help you understand and determine these issues. As you read through these sections, you will start to subliminally consider the nature of each of your expenses and, in turn, whether you will be able to reduce or even eliminate them going forward.

Fixed, Variable and Discretionary Expenses

As you review your expenses, you will discover that you have some costs that remain the same from month to month, such as mortgage or rent payments, car repayments, or insurance premiums. These are your fixed costs. Conversely, you will also notice certain costs that are variable. These are costs that fluctuate based on your spending habits. Personal shopping, buying gifts, and entertainment are all examples of variable costs and, in many cases, increases in variable costs are often due to increased expenditure on discretionary or non-essential items.

Spending is an Emotional Habit!

By all accounts, spending money is a highly emotional activity. Budgeting, on the other hand, is an intellectual one. We are enticed into buying products and services that give us a feeling of improved health, appearance, financial security or otherwise. We buy that expensive coat or that outfit that makes us feel better about ourselves. All too often, however, the emotional desire to feel better gets in the way of financial sense. When this happens too often, or when we spend beyond our means, we can all too quickly find ourselves in financial trouble.

Understanding which costs are flexible and which are variable is important as, more often than not, your savings will come by exercising more control over your variable or discretionary costs.

In the table on the next page, we have included details of a variety of different types of expenses. Some of these are fixed in nature while others are variable in nature. More importantly, some of these expenses will be discretionary expenses. Discretionary expenses are those expenses which you incur which you could really live without. A typical example of a discretionary expense comes in the form of an entertainment expense such as the cost of a concert ticket.

Fixed Expenses Explained

Fixed expenses do not change depending on your consumption of a good or service. A fixed expense is a cost that does not generally change from period to period. Fixed expenses are usually paid on a regular basis, such as week to week, month to month, quarter to quarter or year to year. Examples include rent, mortgages, insurance, pension payments and some utility bills.

Variable Expenses Explained

Variable expenses change depending on how much you consume of a good or service. A variable expense is a cost that can change considerably from period to period, such as weekly, monthly, quarterly or yearly. Examples include heating, fuel, groceries, entertainment, etc.

Type of Expense		
Fixed Expenses	**Variable Expenses**	**Discretionary Expenses**
• Car insurance	• Car repairs and maintenance	• Babysitting
• Car loan payments	• Cleaning supplies and equipment	• Books
• Cell phones	• Daycare	• Cable subscriptions
• Charitable donations	• Electricity	• Children's activities
• Childcare	• Food / Groceries	• Donations
• Garbage collection	• Footwear / Clothing	• Entertainment
• Health insurance	• Gas	• Gifts
• House insurance	• Heating	• Hair care
• Internet	• House repairs and maintenance	• Hobbies
• Life insurance	• Parking	• Holidays
• Loans	• Personal care	• Memberships
• Property taxes	• Pet care	• Newspaper / Magazines
• Rent or mortgage	• Postage	• Restaurants
• Savings	• Prescriptions & Medical	• Sports & other activities
• Telephone	• Credit card	• Tobacco / alcohol
• Transportation		• Toys
• Tuition		
• Water/ Sewerage		

Important Tip

What if I underestimate some of my expenses or leave them out of my records altogether?

First of all, it's not very likely that you are going to be able to pin point every single cent you have spent over a particular period of time. Most of us don't have records that are that detailed. So, for the purposes of getting started with your budget, all you simply need to do is to prepare a list of expenses that is as accurate as you can possibly make it having regard to the information that you have to hand. In doing so, if you capture all of your material expenditures you will be most of the way there. As you implement your budget, you will be able to keep better track of your expenditures and more accurate details will be substituted into your plan as time progresses.

Understanding What Your Finances are Telling You

Now that you have taken the time to review your income and expenditure, you will have determined that either you spend more than you earn or you earn more than you spend. If you earn more that you spend, then well done! Your budgeting exercise should be that little bit easier as you already have a good degree of control over your finances. However, the fact that you are 'in the black' doesn't by any means suggest that you don't need to budget. By paying less for the things you have or need, you will have more disposable income in your pocket to enjoy life more. You may even be able to save or invest the additional money that you save by reducing your expenses.

If you are spending more that you earn, then you really need to be careful. This has the potential to turn into a serious problem as, in order to finance this overspending, you will need to either eat into your savings or borrow money to finance the extra expenditure. Of course, borrowed finance will come at an additional charge in the form of interest payments. This, in turn, will adversely affect your debt position.

Borrowing money to finance your lifestyle can be disastrous. Not alone will it affect your financial position, all too often it can affect your home, family, mental health and relationships. Debt problems are simply best avoided – especially where the incurring of debt in the first instance is not absolutely necessary. You may feel that this assessment is a little over-dramatic. However, when you have exhausted your savings and reached your maximum level of borrowings, you can rest assured that life will not be too rosy when the creditors come knocking on your door looking for money you cannot repay, threatening to take court action or even to contact your employer. When debt spirals out of control, it can affect every aspect of your life.

To avoid these types of problems, you need to take immediate control over your finances. This is where goal setting, reducing costs and budgeting come into play. In the ensuing chapters, we'll show you how to do each of these things, how to monitor your progress and how to stick to the plan!

Understanding What the Budget Spreadsheet is Telling You

In Chapter 1, we introduced you to the budget spreadsheet and each of the individual tabs contained in the spreadsheet. We explained the information contained in each tab and how that information was presented to you in the form of tables, graphs and pie-charts. We also explained how each of the tabs in that spreadsheet relate to each other in order to give you a global view of your actual income and expenses as well as your desired income and expense levels. If you have completed the spreadsheet, a careful examination of the information that it contains will give you an invaluable insight of where your money is going on a daily, weekly and monthly basis and, of course, where you could possibly reduce those expenses.

CHAPTER 3

SETTING GOALS

Chapter Overview

Having gained a valuable insight into your current spending habits, the next thing you need to do is to decide on what you would actually like to be doing with your money. In other words, you need to decide what your financial goals are. You may not of course have the means to achieve them just yet, but that's something we'll look at in the ensuing chapters.

What are Your Budget Goals?

Now that you have a good understanding of your current financial position, and before actually sitting down to create your budget plan, you will need to take some time to consider and establish a clear set of financial goals. It's only by determining your financial objectives that you can formulate and design a plan that will accomplish those objectives. Without setting proper goals, the whole budgeting exercise might seem more like needless restrictions on your financial freedom than an actual means to an end. Consider those targets as the motivation factors and rewards for the effort of making and sticking to your budget plan.

You should begin by making a list of your goals. These may be as simple as paying off a particular debt, saving for a down payment on your first home or as elaborate as creating a property or investment portfolio. The choice is yours. Remember, with proper planning, most realistic goals can be achieved!

Adding Time Frames to Your Goals

Once you have made a list of your goals, the next task will be to allocate appropriate time frames for the achievement of those goals. These time frames will depend on the nature of the goals themselves and the financial resources at your disposal. However, broadly speaking, these time frames can be broken down into long, medium and short-term goals.

When setting goals, many people start with setting short-term goals and then move to setting both medium and long-term goals. This, of course, is a classic mistake. In setting goals, you should always start with the setting of long-term goals. Once you have identified these long-term goals, you should seek to identify the short and medium-terms goals that you will need to accomplish in order to attain these long-term goals. It is only by ensuring that your short and medium-terms goals are aligned with your long-term goals that you can actually ensure that you are doing the right things now to succeed in the long-term.

Long-Term Goals

Long-term goals are often described as goals with a completion date longer than 7 years into the future. These goals are often less clear than shorter or medium-terms goals because the attainment of these goals is often contingent upon the attainment of numerous smaller goals over the short and medium-term. However, the clearer you can be on a long-term goal the more the more likely you are to obtain your objective. It is important therefore to move beyond a simply long-term vision and set down on paper what it is that you actually want. For example, your vision may be to have a comfortable and happy retirement, but purchasing a house on your favorite lake with cash in the next 10 years so that you and your family can enjoy the summers when you retire is a goal.

Long-term goals for your budget could include the following:

- Save for your children's college education.

- Quit your job and start your own business.

- Build a retirement fund.

- Pay off the mortgage early.

- Purchase a new or vacation home.

However, even long-term goals need to be specific!!! Let's re-write the above long-term goals again, but this time making them a little more specific:-

- Save $30,000 by September 2026 to pay for Ann and Sarah's college education.

- Retire from my current job in December 2028 and start my own business in January 2029 as a financial advisor for those approaching retirement.

- Build a retirement fund of $100,000 so that I can retire in December 2035.

- Pay off the $60,000 mortgage on my family home in New York by June 2030.

- Purchase a vacation home for $250,000 by October 2035 so that I can retire and spend time there with my family.

Don't these goals seem a lot more realistic and achievable now that you have added dates and monetary amounts to each? This is the secret of goal setting! Being as specific as possible and adding deadlines for achieving goals is the only way to ensure that you will achieve your goals.

Important Tip

Don't set yourself up for failure. Make your goals as realistic as possible. Then reassess the viability of each of them after you determine how much you can save by cutting-back on your expenses during the next chapter. Remember to be patient – achieving goals takes time and discipline.

Once you've identified your long-term goals, you will have some clear objectives for your budget.

Medium-Term Goals

Medium-term goals can generally be described as goals which take longer than one year to accomplish, but less than seven years. They will include both stand-alone goals and goals which are necessary to achieve in order to accomplish your long-term goals. In formulating medium-term goals, the planning becomes more specific and more critical. This is because, like long-term goals, medium-term goals will need to be broken down into a series of smaller, short-term goals so that they can be achieved and progress monitored. These short-terms goals then become the key to achieving your medium-term goals.

The attainment of medium-term goals can sometimes seem a little daunting as they often appear much more difficult to achieve than short-term goals which sometimes require little real effort. However, it's important to stay focused and committed. You should follow the short-term goals necessary to achieve the medium-term goals. As you complete each short-term goal, you will enforce the belief in your ability to grow and succeed. And as your list of completion dates grow, your motivation and desire will increase.

People often pay much more attention to their short-term goals and neglect their long and medium-term goals. However, it is important to review your long and medium-term goals frequently, so that you don't lose sight of these important objectives and so that your short-term goals are properly aligned to the achievement of these goals.

Short-Term Goals

Opinions vary on what exactly a short-term goal is, but most people view a short-term goal as something that will take less than one year to accomplish. Of course, depending on the type of goal, it may take a lot less time. For example, if your goal is to pay your electric bill in the next few days, then that goal might be very short-term indeed. In many instances, the achievement of short-term goals requires little more that a commitment to booking time in to your schedule to do whatever needs to be done to achieve the goals in question.

As mentioned, short-term goals form a pivotal part of the attainment of both long and medium-term goals. They are the foundation stones upon which these longer term goals are achieved. As a result, they need to be much more specific than medium or long-term goals and must have very specific time frames attached to their accomplishment. To this end, short-term goals can and should be broken down into daily, weekly, monthly and even yearly goals.

Did You Know?

In order for a financial goal to be realistic, it must:

- have a dollar amount attributed to it;

- have a timeframe for its achievement;

- have a realistic possibility of achievement; and

- be measurable.

Setting and achieving daily goals is the foundation of successful achieving. This is where the action takes place, where you do the small things that amount to something bigger and contribute towards the attainment of small, medium and long-term goals. Each day, you should carefully make a list of all of the things that you need to do that day in order to ensure that your goals are being met. These will be the tasks that you need to prioritize.

Once you have decided on your daily goals, the next goals that you will need to focus on will be your weekly goals. These will be designed to help achieve your monthly goals. Your monthly goals, in turn, will form part of the constituent parts of your yearly and short-term goals. In determining your yearly goals, studies have shown that focusing on four to five main goals achieves the most success.

Important Tip

In setting goals, ask yourself what you would need to do in the next year to achieve a specific goal. For example, if you want to save $5,000, you will need to consider what short and medium-term items you may need to cut back on to save that money. Remember, the key is to break all large goals down into small individual goals and to set realistic time frames to achieve each of these smaller goals.

Here are some examples of **short-term goals**:

- Reduce my debt levels by increasing my repayments on my car loan by $50 a month commencing on 30 June 2017.

- Pay for home repairs and renovations worth $8,000 by December 31 2017.

- Pay off medical bills by the end of next week.

- Start saving for the down payment on my vacation home at the end of next month by placing $100 per month into a specific savings account at the end of each calendar month.

- Build a savings account by placing $20 per week into a specific savings account at the end of each week.

Remember, just like long-term and medium-term goals, be sure to attach a specific timetable to short-term goals. This allows you to measure your progress against a specific timeline. A goal without such a timeline is far too open-ended and simply leaves too much room for deviation and failure.

A sample of our Goal Setting Worksheet has been included below with an illustration on how you might achieve a goal to buy a new car. To be clear, we are not suggesting that you run out and buy a new car – particularly a relatively expensive one such as a BMW! We are simply using this as an example of goal setting. In fact, whatever goal you set yourself its achievement should tie in with all your other long, medium and short-term goals. Remember, good planning starts with identifying long-term goals and working your way backwards.

Goal Setting Worksheet

In order to make your goals become a reality, you must write them down. The worksheet below allows you to enter your goals, the duration in which you expect to achieve each goal, whether the goal is a high, medium or low priority and the actions that you need to take in order to attain your goals.

Goal	Duration	Priority	Annual and Monthly Goal Cost	Actions	Motivation Factors
Buy a new Black BMW 320i Sport Plus with full sports trim and red leather seats.	Within 2 years	#1 (High)	$20,000 – payable monthly on finance at $300 per month	- Sell my old car within the next 90 days. Take pictures of the car tonight and place an advert online before the end of the week. - Reduce my existing monthly expenses by $300 per month by doing the following: 1. Stop buying coffee each day before work. *Start time: Tomorrow morning!* 2. Change my mobile phone operator to save $10 per month. *Start time: End of this month following the giving of the required one month cancellation notice!* 3. Cancel the gym membership that I am not currently using. *Start time: Today.* 4. Cycle to work 1 day per week to save on rail fares. *Start time: Monday next.* 5. Reduce entertainment nights from 3 per week to 2 per week. *Start time: End of this week!*	- A BMW is the car of my dreams. I love the way the car handles, the speed that it can achieve, the brand recognition and the feeling of power and control I have when driving one. - I will save on the repair costs that I am already paying on my old car. - My insurance premium will be less - The cost of gasoline will be reduced as the BMW is more fuel efficient than my old car

Exercise 6 – Setting Your Goals

Now that you have details of your current income and expenditure levels, as well as an understanding of goal setting, it's important that you document these goals in your budget worksheet and set out the actions you need to achieve them. The addition of these goals in your worksheet will act as a constant reminder of why you are budgeting in the first place. More importantly, it will help give you some of the motivation needed to stick to your budget. In fact, to re-enforce this motivation, it's a good idea to print some copies of your goal worksheet and place copies in significant places where you will see them – this should keep you motivated and focused.

A copy of the Goal Setting Worksheet is set out on page 120 of this kit and can be downloaded from enodare.com (see page 17 for details).

Complete your worksheet using the following steps:

1. Identify each of your financial goals and write them down in the "Goal" column. Be as clear and descriptive about each of your goals as possible. Don't simply write down "to buy a new car". Write down the make, model, color and any other pertinent details of the car you want. Do this for all of your goals and spend time at it. Research has consistently shown that by being as clear and detailed as possible in describing your goals, you dramatically increase the probability of attaining them.

2. Specify how long you expect it to take to achieve each of your goals. You may need to work backwards on some of these. For example, if you know the cost of achieving your goal is $5,000 and that you can only contribute $100 a month towards reaching this target, you will need 50 months, or 4 years and two months, to accomplish that goal.

3. Decide on a priority level for each of your goals. Use the following priority indicators:-

    #1   =   "High" or "Very important".

    #2   =   "Medium" or "Fairly important".

    #3   =   "Low" or "Not very important".

    #4   =   "None" or "Not important". Items falling in this category are really items that you would like to have but are not that important in the bigger scheme of things such as, for example, a new outfit for the party next weekend.

    By attributing a priority level to each item, you can quickly decide which goals you might want to forsake if your budget hits a 'bump on the road". Alternatively, you can determine

Exercise 6 – Setting Your Goals

which goals to focus on if your current financial position doesn't allow you to pursue all of them at once.

4. In the fourth column, insert the financial amount that the goal will cost to achieve. In addition to setting out the total cost, break this figure down into a monthly amount so that you can allocate an appropriate amount in your monthly budget (which you will prepare later) to meet this cost. Be realistic in identifying how much you can allocate. It may not be possible to achieve all of your goals at once. You should add up the monthly cost of all of your goals so that you can determine whether it is compatible with your overall budget. Remember, that if you are setting aside an amount on a monthly basis to achieve these goals, that amount needs to feature in your budget and, more importantly, your budget must have sufficient scope financially to allow for it!!! If not, you may need to forego a goal for now (this is where priority allocation comes in) or adjust the timeframe for achieving it and the monthly amount required to do so.

5. A goal is of little value unless you can actually achieve it!! In the "Actions" column set out the specific things that you will do to help meet the cost of achieving each goal. There may be a specific sacrifice that you are willing to make in order to achieve a specific goal or indeed several goals. At the end of the day, you will need to make enough financial sacrifices and/or cut-backs as are necessary to achieve your goals and you will need to know how to do that. If you cannot do this, the unfortunate reality is that some or all of your goals are simply not realistic. Remember goals can only be achieved if they are realistic!

6. In order to keep you motivated towards achieving each goal, you should clearly set out motivational factors why you want to achieve each particular goal. How will you benefit from achieving a particular goal? How will you feel? What are the advantages? Add as many reasons as you can. Again, research has shown that by clearly knowing why you want to achieve a particular goal, you will remain more focused on it and more likely to achieve it.

Goal Setting for Couples and Families

If you are part of a couple or a family, you will need to align the goals of your partner and/or your family with your own. There is no point in trying to save for an expensive holiday if your partner is planning on spending any extra savings you make on an elaborate house extension. Sit down with your partner and/or family member, discuss your goals openly and decide on those that you wish to pursue jointly. Then fill out the goals worksheet in the exact same way as suggested above. This time, however, you may need to allocate specific actions to your partner and/or other members of your family as a combined effort will be required from everyone if those particular goals are to be achieved.

In addition to goal setting, it may also be necessary to prepare a combined budget so that the "action" steps are all aligned. We'll discuss this in further detail later.

Review Your Goals Regularly

Both your goals and your ability to attain your goals will change from time to time. This is because our financial circumstances, desires and interests change quite frequently. For this reason, it is recommended that you review your goals on a regular basis, and especially when you are planning to make any significant changes to your budget. Remember, your budget is the means by which you achieve your goals. As such, both must be kept in sync. At the very least, you should review your goals at least every six months or whenever there is a significant change in your financial circumstances.

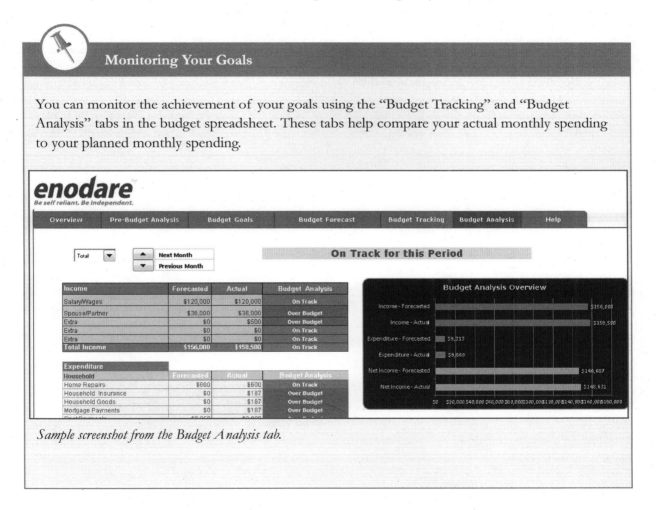

Monitoring Your Goals

You can monitor the achievement of your goals using the "Budget Tracking" and "Budget Analysis" tabs in the budget spreadsheet. These tabs help compare your actual monthly spending to your planned monthly spending.

Sample screenshot from the Budget Analysis tab.

CHAPTER 4

STRATEGIES TO REDUCE EXPENSES & SAVE MONEY

Chapter Overview

A budget provides an insight into where a person spends money, but also helps to identify opportunities for reducing expenses by spending less on budgeted items—not necessarily by cutting them out entirely, but by finding ways to reduce those expenses. This chapter will outline ways to cut costs in a broad variety of areas in order to create more flexibility in a budget and help with achieving the savings goal.

Why Reduce Expenses?

In order to attain the goals that you formulated in the previous chapter, you will most likely need to increase the gap between your income and your expenditure. Of course, the easiest way to do this is by reducing expenses rather than increasing income. The savings that you make from cutting back on your expenses will be used to finance the achievement of your goals. Therefore, in this chapter, we will explore a variety of different ways in which you can reduce your expenses.

Prioritizing Your Expenses

When analyzing your personal financial situation, it's natural that you may find yourself somewhat overwhelmed by the amount of expenses that you discover you have. However, you shouldn't panic. By prioritizing the payment of your various expenses, you will be able to quickly see which expenses you actually need to incur and which you can avoid with a little planning.

Prioritizing your expenses is important and each expense should be given an appropriate priority rating. This ranking could be as simple as 'low', 'medium' or 'high' priority. Once you've done this, you will be able to identify the expenses you can live without and those you cannot. Failing to adequately prioritize expenses is one of the main reasons why budgets fail.

So what should you prioritize first? Well, that's easy - your first consideration should always be towards the basics such as food, medical care and accommodation expenses (such as rental or mortgage repayments). Next you need to consider household expenses such as your electric and gas bills. These are the necessities that you need for your day to day living. Following this, your priorities should be directly related to your needs. Perhaps you need a car to get to work or job interviews? In such cases, expenses like car loans, car maintenance, car insurance and gas could be prioritized higher than others. On the other hand, maybe you can take the subway to work and a car is a luxury expense and therefore should be given a low priority. Maybe you are in a position where creditors have threatened law suits, perhaps in connection with your car or house repayments? If so, the payment of these expenses may then become a higher priority? It may even make more sense to sell your car or other assets to raise the relevant funds? Alternatively, you may simply want to pay off your credit card in order to avoid heavy interest rates. Either way the process of the prioritizing your expenses should not be overlooked and is fundamental to the success of your budget.

While priorities will differ for every individual, your expenses should nonetheless be scrutinized and then prioritized. You may even discover ways to cut back on some of your high priority expenses, for example you could ride your bike to work, move to a cheaper location to lower your rent or even consider if you need your current cell phone plan.

 Exercise 7 - Prioritizing Your Expenses

Prioritizing your expenses is a relatively straightforward exercise. To carry out this exercise, simply extract details of your expenses from your daily, weekly, monthly and annual expense worksheets and add them into the relevant columns in the table below. You will need to give careful thought as to the importance of each of these expenses. If you have used the budget spreadsheet, you will have had the opportunity to select whether each expense was a priority (non-discretionary) expense or not (discretionary) when originally adding details of each expense.

Expense Priority Worksheet					
High Priority Expense		**Medium Priority Expense**		**Low Priority Expense**	
Item	Amount	Item	Amount	Item	Amount

Where to Look for Savings Opportunities

Rarely is there an individual who isn't spending more than necessary in some aspect of their life. Whether it's not shopping for the best deals or wasting energy that drives up bills, there is always some area where we can uncover ways to cut costs.

The best way to find these hidden savings is to review each of the expenses that you listed during the exercises in Chapter 2. Start by looking at the biggest expenses. Shaving even 10 percent off a $200 monthly expense puts $20 back in the budget. Look at the big numbers and then work your way down the list, considering each expense in turn. For each expense, think about how you came up with the cost. Are you using the price you've always paid? Do you know if that's the best price you can get? From credit card and mortgage rates to everyday essentials, there are undiscovered savings that can be found when you know where to look and take the time to look.

You can use the Expense and Debt Reduction Worksheet to document where you can make your savings. Download instructions are set out on Pg 17 of this book.. Remember, the key in this process is to analyze each expense one by one!

Finding Cost Savings

In this section, we're going to provide you with some practical tips on how to save money. We're not going to create an exhaustive list of things you can do to save money, nor will we insist that you adopt each or any particular suggestion that we provide. What we will do however, is give you some insights into some very practical techniques that allow families to reduce expenses and save money each month. However, we must warn you up front - saving money isn't always easy.

Mortgage

If you haven't already refinanced your home to take advantage of a lower interest rate, you could reduce your monthly mortgage payment with as little as a half-percentage point reduction in the rate. Put the savings into a retirement fund or use it to pay off the mortgage sooner. Shop around to find the best deals from mortgage companies including your current provider as it might be willing to offer a more competitive rate/product just to keep your business.

Electric

There are many ways to save money on electricity throughout the home.

- Turn off lights.
- Unplug items that are not regularly in use (e.g., coffee maker, computer, printer, toaster, television, cell phone charger, etc). Even when not turned on, these items continue to draw energy from the outlet.
- Use energy-saving compact fluorescent lights (CFLs) instead of incandescent bulbs, particularly in fixtures that are used frequently or have multiple lights. A 60-watt

incandescent can be replaced with a 13-watt CFL without sacrificing light. CFLs last up to ten times longer than ordinary bulbs and use 75 percent less electricity. An Energy Star compact fluorescent light bulb, for example, can save you $30 over its lifetime in electric costs, and pay for itself in about 6 months.

- Install and use ceiling fans as an alternative to air conditioners, which consume more energy.
- Choose energy-efficient appliances when it's time to replace the existing ones.
- Use the microwave instead of the stovetop, especially for small meals. Microwaves use about 84 percent less electricity.
- Run the dishwasher only when it is full. Partial loads waste water and the electricity required to heat the water.
- Wash laundry in cold water instead of warm or hot. Heating the water accounts for 80 to 90 percent of the energy used to run the appliance.
- Lower the temperature on the electric water heater and save three to five percent in electricity for every 10 degrees. Ideally, a water heater should be set at 120°F. An electric water heater uses the most energy of any household appliance, about 2,400 kilowatt hours (kwh) per year; compare this to a refrigerator (700 kwh) and dishwasher (200 kwh) and you can see the importance of paying attention here.
- Use dimmers and sensors on lights to control energy use.

Heating

The amount paid for heating the space and the water in a home amounts to about 63 percent of the annual utility costs, so this is a prime area to identify savings.

- Shop around with other providers to see if there are more competitive heating fuel rates available.

- Investigate the cost and return on investment for changing to a different type of heating fuel that might be less expensive. Some suppliers offer incentives to switch so the initial cost could be zero and will start you saving right away.

- Check doors, windows, floors, walls, ceilings, and electrical outlets for drafts that allow heat (and heating dollars) to escape.

- Wrap insulation around the electric water heater and pipes to prevent heat from escaping. If your electric or gas water heater was built before 2004, then adding an insulating jacket can save you around 10% annually on your water heating bill.

- Close the fireplace flue damper when not being used.

- Have the insulation and air ducts inspected by a professional.

- Replace filters on air conditioners and furnaces once a month. A dirty filter reduces the efficiency of the unit.

- Make sure that warm-air registers and baseboard radiators are free from obstructions, like furniture, carpet, and draperies.

- In cooler weather, open the oven door after use to allow the remaining heat to warm the kitchen.

- Install a programmable thermostat that lowers the interior temperature at specified times. Turning back the heat by 10°F for eight hours a day (overnight or during the day when you're out of the house) can save up to 10 percent on heating costs per year. By properly setting your programmable thermostats, you could save about $180 a year on your home heating costs.

- By lowering the temperature on your thermostat by 1 degree in the winter time, you can expect to save between 2 and 5% on your home heating costs.

- By raising the temperature on your thermostat by just 1 degree in the summer time, you can expect to save 2 to 5% on your air conditioning bills.

- Contact your heating fuel supplier to determine if you can save money by prepaying on estimated fuel usage.

- Have your home's furnace or boiler serviced once every two years. By doing so, you can expect to save as much as 10% on your annual home heating bills.

Water Bills

Changing the way that you use your water supplies can also have an impact on your savings.

- It is estimated that the average household could save approximately 2,500 gallons of water per annum by simply using a low flow shower. Not alone will this yield around $60 in savings per year on your water bill, but it should also help you save money on your water heating bills.

- By purchasing a 'Watersense' toilet, you could save about 4,000 gallons of water which translates in to approximately $90 per year on your water bill. Of course, the cost of purchasing the toilet needs to be measured against the expected savings.

- By installing a faucet aerator in each bathroom in your house, the average household could expect to save around 500 gallons of water each year as well as make some savings on its water heating bills.

Insurance

While insurance is essential, there are ways to spend less without compromising the valuable coverage.

- If you haven't already consolidated your policies with one insurer, you might realize significant savings by doing so. Contact your agent to discuss this option.

- Shop around with reliable insurers to determine if you can obtain better rates.

- Look for insurers that offer discounts on car insurance for safe drivers (no violations or accident claims), honor students, automatic or pre-payment of premiums, and for vehicles equipped with anti-theft devices, anti-lock brakes, and passive restraints (airbags and motorized seat belts). You could also save about 10 percent on your car insurance by completing a driver safety course.

- Paying the annual premium all at once, instead of monthly or quarterly, can provide a saving. Check with your insurer to see if there is a discount for payment in full.

- People who work from home might be eligible for discounted rates on car insurance because of the reduced amount of vehicle use.

- Security systems like fire and burglar alarms and sprinklers can save a homeowner as much as 20 percent on home insurance premiums, but even installing deadbolt locks and simple alarms can realize a saving.

- Increase the home insurance policies' deductibles. The money saved on premiums might be more than enough to cover the added cost if you need to file a claim.

- If you currently have specific coverage for prescriptions on your medical insurance, consider whether the cost will actually save money in the long run. With the reduced cost and increased availability of generic medications and pharmacy discount programs that lower prescription prices, you might save money by opting out of the additional coverage.

Telephone

Between landlines and cell phones—with data and messaging plans attached—these bills can add a heavy weight to a budget's bottom line.

- Review your last three phone bills to determine your usage. You might be paying for more minutes than you actually need. If you haven't been using your monthly allotment of minutes, downgrading your plan—which should be capable of being done without incurring a penalty—can save you money.

- Watch out for roaming charges that apply when making or receiving calls outside your designated area. Some carriers that offer low-cost rate plans have hidden caveats about roaming charges. Depending on the carrier—whether or not they have coverage in certain regions—roaming charges might apply and the fees can quickly add up. Be clear on what you're paying for.

- A family plan can save money when there are multiple users on an account—even if the members are not living under the same roof.

- Contact your provider and ask for an explanation of the various service fees charged to your account. You might have a recurring fee for a service you never subscribed to or even a ringtone you're no longer using. You might have downloaded an app and unwittingly subscribed to a monthly service or become the victim of identity theft. Some carriers will credit your account for these charges if it's determined that those services were unauthorized.

- Compare packages with other phone service providers. Be sure you know about the penalties for cancelling an existing contract too soon before committing to a new agreement elsewhere.

- Because cell phone carriers have become even more competitive, the rates currently charged for plans today might be less than the same program you signed up for a year or two ago. Ask your carrier to extend the same value to you, as a loyal customer. While they rarely publicize such options, carriers will make an effort to keep customers who have remained in good credit standing so you might discover some savings here.

- Remember that calling a "toll-free" number from a cell phone is not a free call. You will pay for the time you spend on the call. Whenever possible, use a landline for these calls.

- Determine if you actually need to maintain both a cell phone and a landline. More and more consumers are cancelling their landlines, using only their cells and taking advantage of the free mobile-to-mobile calling feature offered by many providers.

Cable Television

According to the U.S. Bureau of Labor and Statistics, the average American spends an astronomical $954 per year on cable television services. The cable bill is therefore often a great place to shave costs.

- Contact the other cable and satellite television service providers to learn if there are more cost-effective packages than your current package.

- Some providers offer bundled packages on cable, phone and internet services. Check to see if you could make some savings by having a combined package, but understand the limits of the package (introductory offers expire after three or six months).

- Check your provider's website for promotions offered to new subscribers and then call the company to ask for the same offer to be extended to loyal customers like you.

- Review the cable bill to look for extras that could be eliminated, like premium channels, high-definition, and additional cable boxes or digital video recorders (DVRs).

- Look at sites like Hulu.com where you can watch television shows and movies for free. By hooking up your computer to your television, you can stream the programs to the big screen.

- Rather than paying for on-demand viewing, take a short trip to a video kiosk where you can rent a movie for about one dollar a day. Netflix.com subscribers can also choose from thousands of movies to watch on demand at no extra charge.

Internet Service

Like cell phone and cable television, having an internet service seems like a necessity so we pay for it, but this monthly cost might have some options for savings.

- As mentioned, bundling your internet service with cable television and/or telephone services can provide lower rates overall.

- If you are paying extra for high-speed internet, consider downgrading to a slower service. Depending on your use, you might not even notice the difference.

- Ask yourself if you need the internet in your home. With free high-speed internet "hot spots" readily available in many public locations, you might be able to utilize nearby internet access and save the money on the in-home bill.

- If you live in a condominium or apartment complex with close proximity to neighbors, you can share internet access via a wireless router, as long as your computers have wireless connectivity. Speak to your neighbors about sharing the cost of the service.

Credit Cards

Having credit is a privilege, but it can come with mounting costs. Consider the tips below for reducing the cost of having and using credit cards.

- Avoid finance charges by paying the balance in full each month. Not only will this save the extra expense, but this payment history will increase your credit score, which can save money in the future on other loans and credit lines through lower interest rates that are offered to people with higher credit ratings.

- Pay attention to the interest rate charged by your credit card issuer. Shop around for better rates, starting with the current credit card company. Some will offer a lower interest rate to credit-qualified customers just to retain them. Go to Bankrate.com to compare credit card rates.

- Pay the monthly bill as soon as you receive the statement. Interest is compounded daily, so every day that you wait will cost more money. A $3,000 balance on a card with a 29 percent interest rate accrues $74 in interest in just one month. If you pay the bill two weeks before the end of those 30 days, you can save $40.63.

- Do not pay a membership fee for a credit card. If you currently have one (or more), look for a credit card offer with a low or no interest introductory offer. Transfer the balance on the fee-paid card to the new one and pay off the balance without the additional fee. Be sure not to charge additional purchases to the new card because the new charges will likely carry a higher interest rate.

- Choose credit card companies that offer rebates or points for the types of rewards you want. For example, if you rarely fly, you don't need air travel miles, but you might use bonus points offered by another card in the form of savings on gasoline or purchases at stores and restaurants that you frequent.

Automobile Cost Savings

Owning a car is a large expense. Between car payments, insurance, maintenance, gasoline, and registration fees, it's worth looking more closely at your vehicle to find savings opportunities.

- When considering a new car, weigh the cost of purchasing against leasing. The sale price is the best negotiated deal, while a lease is calculated only on the amount that the vehicle depreciates over the lease term. Because you're financing a lesser amount with a lease, the payment will be much less than a car loan. However, you don't have equity in the vehicle and will not own it at the end of the term.

- Drive your existing car for longer and hold off on making that upgrade until necessary. Most cars depreciate in value quicker when they are newer than later in their workable life. Nowadays, most cars can provide about 200,000 miles of driving before needing replacement. So hold off on upgrading unless you really need to.

- Don't limit your choices to local auto dealerships. Search the web for the best deals on a vehicle. In this competitive market, dealers are willing to deliver a car across a long distance in order to make a sale.

- Ask about manufacturer incentives, like instant rebates and zero percent financing.

- Use Craigslist (*www.craigslist.com*) and your local paper to advertise your used vehicle. Before buying a car, check out loan rates, both locally and online. Credit unions often have lower interest rates than banks and you can become a member with as little as a $10 deposit.

- Talk to your insurance agent about premiums for different types of makes and vehicles (compact, SUV, truck, etc) to determine if there are cost savings to choosing one vehicle over another.

- Calculate the annual gasoline cost for each car you're considering to see if it fits with your budget.

- Follow the recommended regular maintenance—like keeping air filters clean, properly inflating tires, keeping the engine tuned, buying the correct octane, changing the oil regularly and rotating tires. These adjustments not only extend the life of the vehicle, but also improve gas mileage and reduce repair costs in the long run.

- Look for a prepaid gasoline card that offers a reduced per-gallon rate.

- Walk instead of driving your car short distances! This will not only extend the life of your car but possibly also your own! Not to mention keeping your travel costs down.

Groceries Cost Savings

Food is a necessity, but this is an area of the budget where we can often find significant savings that are easily overlooked. Here are some ways to reduce your weekly grocery expense.

- Clip and use coupons. They are readily available in newspapers, magazines, and online. The Sunday paper often includes coupon inserts. The savings can be worth more than the cost of the newspaper. You can also find coupons online at Coupons.com, RedPlum.com, AllYou.com, and CouponMom.com. Clip out the coupons for items that you buy and organize them by the grocery store aisles where the items are found. This makes it easier to find the coupon you need when you're shopping in the store. Manufacturers often run sales on items for which they currently issue coupons, so if you find a coupon in the Sunday paper, expect to find it on sale somewhere and use the coupon in conjunction with the sale for maximum value.

- If the store has a discount or rewards card, get one and keep it with you to get the best deals.

- Browse the supermarket flyers in advance. Learn where the items you want are on sale and create a list. You don't need to spend a lot of time going from one store to another. Determine one or two that offer the best value and build your shopping list and trip around those stores.

- Plan ahead. Don't go into a supermarket without a list or you will end up buying more than you need. Plan a week's worth of meals and create your list of ingredients from those menus.

- Shop from your cupboards and freezer. We often build up stores of food items that are pushed to the back of the cabinets and freezer. Use these ingredients before buying more.

- Use leftovers. When planning meals, think about how to turn leftovers into another meal or two. You'll create more value, both in terms of the money spent on the ingredients and the time to prepare the meals.

- Read the unit price label. Buying larger quantities doesn't necessarily mean you're getting a lower unit cost.

- Limit your fresh produce choices to in-season fruits and vegetables because they are usually priced lower due to the abundant availability.

- Use less expensive cuts of meat and poultry. Cooking them in crock pots or in stews keeps them tender. Chicken thighs are inexpensive, meaty, and flavorful.

- Buy lunch foods that you can take with you in order to avoid the expense of eating out.

- Opt for buying the store's brand, which is often less expensive than national brands (because of savings in advertising and packaging costs) and comparable in quality.

- Calculate the cost of ingredients versus purchasing a prepared meal to determine the best value. When a store is having a sale on rotisserie chickens, for example, it's often less expensive than buying and roasting a chicken yourself, and you can potentially get more than one meal from it.

- Reduce the amount of bottled water that you purchase. Twenty years ago, people would have laughed at the thought of buying bottled water, now it is commonplace. Buy a simple container, keep it clean, bottle your own water, and start saving money.

- Grow your own vegetables. It doesn't take an expert to grow basic vegetables such as tomatoes, cucumbers, green beans and peppers in your own backyard.

 Did You Know?

Cutting out a daily $2.50 morning treat reduces your annual expenditure by $625 per year!

Personal Care Cost Savings

From clothing to personal hygiene to hair care to over-the-counter medications, you might be able to trim your monthly expenses by following some simple guidelines.

- Review your clothing expenses. If you consistently purchase new clothes each month, think about cutting back here. You can often "shop your closet" and create new outfits by matching up different pieces that you've never paired before. Also pay attention to sales. Some department stores offer discounts on a certain day of the week, which might afford more savings. Sign up for the e-mailings from your favorite stores to be alerted of upcoming sales and receive discount offers.

- Buy clothing in styles and colors that are less trendy and use accessories to create new looks.

- Many items that are marked "Dry Clean Only" can be washed at home; the label instruction is protection for the manufacturer, not a hard and fast rule. Use a home dry cleaning kit (available in supermarkets and discount department stores). Most polyester fabrics can be machine washed on the delicate cycle or hand washed. Some wool can be cleaned by putting them in the dryer on low heat with a dryer sheet. When shopping for clothing, choose items that do not require dry cleaning.

- Buy health and beauty items at discount department stores, not the supermarket. Although it might be more convenient, you are also likely to pay more for each item (unless it's on sale). Also look for "buy 1, get 1" special offers and bonus packs, and use coupons.

- Rather than purchase the expensive cosmetics in upscale department stores, opt for the brands found in the pharmacies and discount stores. Beauty editors have done comparisons and often prefer the less expensive choices.

- Shampoo your hair every other day. Not only will you double the life of a bottle of shampoo, but your hair will be healthier because shampooing can take away the hairs natural oils.

- Give yourself a home manicure or pedicure.

- Stretch out the time between visits to a hairdresser or shop around for a less expensive stylist.

Entertainment Cost Savings

Living with a budget doesn't mean entertainment is a thing of the past. Discover ways to enjoy leisure time without over-spending.

- Dining out can be a significant expense. Cut back on restaurant dining and experiment with new recipes at home. Make it a family occasion to plan menus, shop for groceries, and cook together.

- Rather than purchase gourmet coffee at Starbucks, invest in a Tassimo or Keurig coffeemaker and brew your choice of coffee to take with you, for about 70 cents a cup. If you buy one cup of coffee per day, you could recoup the cost of the machine in less than one month with the savings.

- Subscribe to websites like Groupon.com and LivingSocial.com and receive daily offers that can save 50 percent or more on restaurants, shopping, live entertainment, attractions, spa treatments, travel, and more.

- Purchase an entertainment coupon book. For about $10 to $15, you can take advantage of rate discounts and two-for-one offers.

- Some associations—AARP, AAA, and many motor clubs, for example— offer entertainment discounts for members. Public libraries often have discounted passes for museums.

- If you enjoy live theatre, volunteer at performances and enjoy them for free.

- Look for discount days at popular attractions.

- Borrow movies and books from the library rather than purchasing them.

- Have a "Game Night" with family and friends.

- Purchase holiday and party decorations at a dollar store rather than a party center.

- Rent video games rather than buying them.

- Review your membership fees. If you're not taking advantage of a health club or yoga studio, for example, cancel the membership.

- Evaluate your subscription expenses. Are you actually reading those newspapers and magazines? If not, cancel them. Many can be viewed online for little or no cost. Conversely, if there's a publication you regularly purchase at newsstands, buy a subscription and save money off the full newsstand rate.

Travel Cost Savings

One of your goals might be to save for a vacation, or you might have travel expenses as a monthly budgeted item. Consider ways to use those dollars more carefully.

- Purchase airline tickets as far in advance as possible to get the best rate. Airlines will offer a limited amount of seats at reduced rates, but once they're sold, expect to pay significantly more.

- When comparing airfare costs, factor in the baggage fees to be sure you're actually saving money.

- Shop around for the best rates on airfare, car rentals, and hotels.

- Verify your car rental insurance with your insurance company before renting a car. In many cases, it may make sense to decline the insurance offered by car rental companies such as the collision damage waiver.

- Hotel Rooms - book the hotel along with your flight or as part of a vacation package. Use discounts offered by travel club memberships such as AAA when booking your hotel

- Look into discounts from employers and associations (e.g., AAA, AARP).

- Browse eBay and Craigslist for people who are selling tickets or vacation packages at a discount.

- If you can be flexible on travel dates, you can save money. Airlines typically charge less to fly midweek than on weekends, and if you can tolerate plane changes or layovers, the fare is lower than a direct flight. Also, cruise lines offer deep discounts on leftover cabins a week or two before the sail date.

- Use a credit card that offers travel rewards to build up your points.

- Stay with the same hotel chain whenever you travel and accrue rewards points toward free nights.

- Consider whether you need to purchase the travel insurance which is offered by most airlines when you purchase flights. You may already have similar insurance in place. In fact, travel insurance regularly comes included with credit cards. Check the terms and conditions of your card!

- When driving, map out a route to avoid tolls, as long as it's not so far out of the way that you're using more gas.

- Theme parks offer discounts on multiple-day passes, but if you're not going to need more days, don't pay for them. The money saved by not purchasing the extra day for a family can fund another excursion.

- Food and beverages are expensive at theme parks. Pack your own snacks. Freeze bottled water the night before your visit and carry it with you to have cold water for most of the day as the ice thaws.

- Park a little farther from popular attractions for lower parking rates.

- Ask hotel employees where to find the best values on dining, shopping, and attractions.

- Use public transportation instead of taxis.

- Car rental agencies not located at airports sometimes have lower rates, so do some research before choosing.

Gift Shopping Cost Savings

All the gifts purchased for holidays, birthdays, anniversaries, weddings, graduations, and showers add up to a significant expense, particularly at Christmas time. Here are some ways to make gift-giving more affordable.

- Set limits on gifts, both on the price of the gift and how many you give. Talk to friends and family members about reducing the gift swapping. Chances are, they are feeling the strain as well.

- Purchase gifts in advance when you find a good sale. Make a note on a calendar as a reminder that you have already purchased the gift.

- Purchase gift cards at a discount at PlasticJungle.com or GiftCardGranny.com. If the card has an odd amount, like $28.79, take it to the store and ask to have the amount transferred to two cards: $25 and $3.79 so that the gift recipient doesn't know you purchased the card at a discount from a reseller.

- Make gifts. From baked goods to gift baskets to handcrafts, you can find ways to economize with hand-made presents.

- Frame a photo or souvenir using a store-bought frame. For less than $10, you can give a very personal gift.

- Look for deals on eBay and Craigslist.

Debt Consolidation

In addition to reducing expenses, many of us may also need to consider debt consolidation. Debt consolidation involves taking out one loan with a view to paying off a number of existing loans. These existing loans may be made up of personal loans, motor loans, bank overdrafts, credit card balances, hire purchase loans and a variety of other types of loans. Debts are usually consolidated in this manner in order to secure a lower interest rate, a fixed interest rate or for the convenience of servicing only one loan.

While many loans advanced for the purpose of debt consolidation are unsecured, some lenders will seek to secure the loans against tangible assets such as property. The provision of collateral or security in this manner may allow you to secure a more favorable interest from the lender due to the reduced risk to which it is exposed. However, it is important to remember that if you default in the repayment of a secured loan, the lender will usually be entitled to take possession of and sell the secured asset. You should therefore take the time to ensure that you are in a sufficient financial position to meet the repayments on the secured loan before accepting it.

In some instances, debt consolidation companies may be willing to purchase one or more of your existing loans from the current lenders where there is a real risk that you will default in the repayment of that loan. Usually, the loan can be purchased for a percentage of the amount owed. For example, if you owe say $10,000 to a lender, the debt consolidation company may be able to buy the entire debt from the current lender for $6,000. The existing lender is paid $6,000 and writes off the balance as bad debt. The debt consolidation company will have the right to recover the full $10,000 from you. However, in many cases, they can pass on some of the benefit to you. So, for example, they could reduce your overall loan to $8,000. By receiving the full amount of $8,000 over time, they will make a full $2,000 profit. Of course, they may also make an additional amount on the interest rate they charge.

A prudent debtor should therefore shop around for debt consolidators who will pass along some of the savings or profits that they will make.

Important Tip

Debt consolidation could affect your ability to discharge certain debts in bankruptcy. If you think that there is a possibility that you will become bankrupt after consolidating your debt, speak to your lawyer before consolidating your debt.

Debt consolidation is generally only advisable where the overall effect is to reduce the level of interest you are paying on your existing borrowings. As credit cards and hire purchase schemes tend to carry much higher interest rates than personal loans, debt consolidation is often used to refinance these particular forms of debt. You should take your time to understand the exact figures involved before accepting a debt consolidation loan.

Alternatives to Debt Consolidation

While debt consolidation does seem to provide a good solution to those who find themselves drowning in a sea of debt, evidence shows that many of those who avail of debt consolidation tend to rack up more credit card debt even before the debt consolidation loan is paid off. As such, depending on your spending habits and discipline other options may be more suitable for you. Some of these options are listed below.

Debt Management Plans

A debt management plan is an informal agreement that is made between you and your creditors. In essence, you will agree on revised payment terms with your creditor to ensure that the debt is repaid. In many cases, the creditor may agree lower interest payments with a view to ensuring that the principal element of the debt is repaid in full. Alternatively, your creditor may agree to defer interest payments until the end of the loan, at which point the interest will become payable in full. The deferral of interest in this manner will mean that you have smaller monthly repayments.

It should however be remembered that, as the agreement is often informal, the creditor can renege on his agreement at any time and call for the debt to be repaid in the pre-agreed manner. Creditors are most likely to do this if you fail to keep up with the revised payment structure or if there is a serious risk of your bankruptcy.

There are many debt advisory companies out there that can help you restructure your debt. If you choose to engage one to act as an intermediary between you and your creditors, be sure to choose a company that has been in business for a suitable length of time and has a good reputation within the market. Remember also to check their fee structure.

Individual Voluntary Arrangements

An individual voluntary arrangement (or an IVA as it's often called) is a formal written agreement made between you and one of your creditors. Under the terms of the agreement, you will agree to make revised monthly payments to your creditor for a specific period of time. During that period, the interest on the repayments is frozen so that all of the payment is diverted to paying off the principal of the debt owing. When the new repayment period comes to an end, the balance of the debt together with interest is usually written off.

IVAs are suitable for people who, when regard is taken of their overall financial position, have a realistic possibility of repaying the debt that is owing or at least a substantial part of it. These arrangements are generally not suitable for people who are clearly heading for bankruptcy. Negotiating IVA arrangements generally requires professional support as the matters involved can be complex. You should therefore speak to your financial advisor before approaching your creditors.

Full & Final Settlements

In some instances, it may be possible for you to offer a large amount in full and final settlement of an existing debt. It you have received a once off payment such as a redundancy payment, an inheritance or the proceeds of sale of a large asset, it may be possible to offer a lump sum to a creditor in full and final settlement of all monies due and owing to him. The lump sum will be offered on the basis that the balance of the amount due (including interest) is written off in full. If you have been experiencing financial difficulties and the creditor is aware of that, then he may be more likely to accept your proposal. However, as you would expect, these types of negotiation can be tricky particularly where you don't have a full understanding of the creditor's business or the margins he is making. As such, it is again recommended that you avail of the services of your financial advisor who is probably much more accustomed to dealing with these types of matters or, if not, can put you in contact with someone that is.

Remember, the goal here is to reduce debt so that you can ultimately focus on getting your financial affairs and budget in order. So, leave it to the professionals where they are better placed to deal with matters.

Bankruptcy

If you have exhausted all methods for controlling your debt, you may wish to consider declaring yourself bankrupt. This is a process by which all your debts will be legally cleared. However, it is not without its consequences and, as such, you should only make a decision to declare yourself bankrupt after you have taken appropriate professional advice.

Debt Counseling

Finally, if your spending habits are completely out of control, you may wish to consider debt counseling. This is like any other form of counseling except that the focus will be on understanding and dealing with your spending habits and your thoughts about money and debt generally. Again, expert advice will be required here and it will not come without fees of its own.

Selling Things You Don't Need!

If you have an abundance of assets around the house that you don't use or need, and you have debts that you need to clear or expenditures that you need to finance, then you should consider selling some of these assets in order to help keep down your debt levels and balance the books. Maybe you have a few stocks that you don't care too much for, or a bicycle or motorcycle that has sat in the garage unused for a while. Maybe you have clothes, books, CDs, DVDs, etc that you could consider selling on websites such as eBay or maybe even sell an old phone on www.mobilevaluer.com. Give it some thought, it may provide a good solution, if only a part solution, to balancing your finances.

Tracking Your Savings Success

Just as we need to monitor our budgets, we should pay equal attention to our savings success. Document the savings earned by using coupons on a shopping trip. The receipts will usually feature that figure so you can enter it onto a savings ledger. A great way to leverage such savings is to actually take that amount and put it in your savings account. If you save $12.62 with coupons and instant rebates, put that amount of cash in an envelope or savings jar until you can get to the bank. In this way, those savings become more than something on paper—it's dollars and cents for shopping smart.

Living with a budget can be rewarding, and the savings game can be even more entertaining. Use savings efforts to motivate you to keep connected with your goals. We'll discuss more on living with your budget in Chapter 7.

Exercise 8– Expense and Debt Reduction Worksheet

In this exercise, you will be required to consider all of the different ways in which you can reduce your current expense and debt levels. While we have listed many of the potential ways in which you can do this in the previous pages of this chapter, it's now time for you to apply some of the techniques that you have learned to your own personal circumstances. In this regard, you will need to evaluate each of the expenses that you listed in your Expense Worksheets one by one and set out details of what you will do in order to try and reduce these debts. This debt reduction exercise is one of the most important exercises that you will carry out in preparing your budget. However, it is not sufficient just to prepare a list of what you can do. You must be proactive and make the necessary appointments and phone calls that need to be made in order to get the ball rolling.

Remember – you should never leave the site of making a goal without taking the first action that is required in order for you to attain that goal. That may be a phone call, email or otherwise. Ensure you take that vital first step and, if possible, do it immediately after completing this exercise.

Expense and Debt Reduction Worksheet – Download Instructions

A copy of the Expense and Debt Reduction Worksheet is set out on page 124 of this kit and can be downloaded from enodare.com (see page 17 for details).

CHAPTER 5

MANAGING DEBT AND CREDIT

Chapter Overview

Managing the payment of debt is a key factor in successfully maintaining your finances. This chapter will provide some useful tips on managing debt, handling credit and improving your credit score.

In this chapter, we will examine some of the more commonly used debt and credit facilities such as loans, credit cards, overdrafts, etc. The manner in which you manage each of these facilities affects your overall 'credit rating' or 'credit score'. When these ratings are affected adversely, you may find it difficult to obtain certain financial facilities. Even where you are successful in being granted a facility, the cost of that facility might be a lot higher than the cost paid by someone with a better credit rating than you. It is for this reason that you need to understand how these facilities work, how the lending institutions assess whether you should be given access to them, how you can get the best deal when purchasing them and more importantly, whether you actually need them at all.

Debt Financing and Credit

In order to finance the purchase of goods and services, most people will either use cash, debt or credit. Understanding how to manage each of these forms of payment method is crucial to ensuring that we maintain control over our finances. The management of cash is perhaps the most straightforward of these methods. Money comes in and money goes out in what is virtually a dollar for dollar exchange. In fact, the preparation of the budget spreadsheets and/or the expenditure worksheets should give you a clear understanding of what's involved in cash management. However, the management of debt and credit on the other hand is a much more complex challenge. For that reason, we will look at both debt and credit in much more detail in the ensuing sections.

Debt and Credit Explained

Do you know the difference between "credit" and "debt"? Credit is the ability to buy something with the promise to pay for it later. Debt, on the other hand, is what somebody gets (or gets into) when they use credit to make purchases.

What is Credit?

In financial terms, credit can be defined as the <u>ability</u> to obtain goods or services before payment, based on the <u>trust</u> that payment will be made in the future. Credit needs to be distinguished from debt which is the amount actually owing on foot of the credit that has been advanced. However, in practice the terms are often (incorrectly) used interchangeably.

The most common types of credit facilities include mortgages, personal loans, credit cards and hire purchase or installment arrangements. When availing of credit it is important to consider the interest rates associated with the credit, the repayment terms and also the overall impact it will have on your budget.

There are two main types of credit:

- **Fixed-payment credit (i.e. loans)** – This is a fixed loan amount that will be borrowed in full and repaid, usually with interest, in fixed amounts on specific dates. The most common types of fixed-payment credit facilities include home loans, mortgages, personal loans and customer loans.

- **Revolving credit** – With revolving credit, the lending institution gives you a facility where you can borrow as much as you wish up to a specific limit. As the credit is revolving, if you borrow less than the limit, you will be able to access the unused credit that remains at any time you wish. When a repayment is made against outstanding credit, more credit is then freed up for future purchases. For example if you have a credit limit of $600 on your credit card and purchase $200 worth of goods, you will then have $400 worth of credit remaining. If you payback $100, you will then have $500 worth of credit available to you.

What is Debt?

Simply put, debt is the amount of money that a person has borrowed from a lender. In time, the borrower will need to repay that debt (often called a loan) to the lender together with interest. Interest can be described as a percentage payment based on the amount of debt borrowed and represents the fees (or part of them) payable to the lender for making the debt available to the borrower in the first instance.

While debt can certainly be very beneficial when used in the right way, many people have trouble managing debt and find themselves under increased pressure to meet the weekly, monthly or annual repayments of that debt. As a result, the management of personal debt remains a very major factor in personal finances.

If you are contemplating using debt as a source of finance, you should carefully consider the amount you are borrowing, the duration for which you are borrowing the money, the interest rate on the debt, the affordability of the periodical repayments, whether there are any other fees payable in connection with the debt (such as arrangement fees) and the penalties associated with late payments or failure to meet a repayment in its entirety when due. Default interest payments are typically charged on late payments until such time as they are made. These interest rates can be extremely high and, in some cases, punitive.

The repayment of debt is an extremely important element of budget planning particularly as most people have significant borrowings of some description – be they in the form of a mortgage, car loan or otherwise. Because of the impact that debt can have on our lives, a considered approach to borrowing should always be taken before incurring debt.

When considering using debt as a source of finance, it is often useful to consider that debt incurred for the purpose of financing your "wants" is less desirable than debts incurred to finance your "needs". Debt incurred for the purpose of financing your needs can be referred to as 'desirable debt'. This could include items such as loans for a college education or a mortgage for a family home. Even if debt is of the desirable type, you should not borrow without properly considering how much you actually need.

In deciding this, you need to ask yourself whether you need to or even should borrow the entire amount or whether you should perhaps save for the deposit for the house you desire, work a part-time job to partially fund college, etc. This all boils down to discipline in managing your finances.

Did You Know?

Paying off debt quickly can reduce the amount you have to pay in the long-term by reducing the amount of interest payable on the debt.

Principal Sources and Categories of Debt

Personal debt can take many forms. Below is a list of some of the main sources of personal debt that you are likely to encounter.

Residential Mortgages:	One of the largest sources of debt for the average person is that created by residential mortgages. These are loans which are taken out to purchase properties which are secured against the properties themselves. While secured loans of this type may allow you obtain a

lower rate of interest on the borrowings, there is always the risk that if you fail to pay the borrowings back, the lender may be able to take possession of and sell the secured property.

These types of mortgages were a significant contributing factor in the U.S. credit crisis, and the pressure this debt has put on borrowers with falling home values has been widely publicized. In fact, according to the Federal Reserve Board of Governors, the total amount of mortgage debt outstanding hit approximately $14.29 trillion by the end of 2016, up almost $1 trillion from 2012. Fortunately, those debt levels are holidng relatively stable year on year.

Revolving Home Loans:

This type of credit is similar to the revolving credit discussed above. The only real difference is that, as the name suggests, the borrowings are usually secured against a property.

The January 2009 Economic Report of The President indicated that revolving home equity credit outstanding in the United States at the time amounted to $577.8 billion. According to the Federal Reserve Board of Governors' most recent G.19 report issued in November 2017, that amount has now reduced to $398 billion.

Credit Cards:

This is a card issued by a financial institution which gives the holder an option to borrow funds, usually at a point of sale such as in a store or online. These funds are usually borrowed with high interest rates and, as such, are primarily used for short-term financing. Credit card debt is one of the most common forms of debt in the U.S. and is perhaps the form of debt that people find the most difficult to manage given its ease of access.

Student Loans:

These are loans taken out by students to fund their educational and living needs while studying. These loans can be significant and can often take years to repay.

Automobile Loans:

As the name suggests, these are loans which are taken out to purchase an automobile. The average amount borrowed under an automobile loan in the U.S. was $27,000 in 2014 moving to $30,000 in 2017.

Small Business Loans:

While these types of loans are typically business related, many of the borrowers of these loans are in fact self-employed individuals rather than corporations. In addition, many small business loans to corporations are guaranteed by individuals. That means that those individuals could be obliged to repay the loans given to the corporation if it doesn't do so.

Payday Advances: These are loans taking out by borrowers to help meet current expenses until they receive their next pay check. These types of loans tend to be small, averaging around $300 per loan but with interest rates of anything up to and over 1000% per annum.

Installment Purchase Plans: These plans typically enable consumers to avail of low interest rates when purchasing specific assets such as TVs, laundry machines, etc. Once purchased, the asset is paid for in weekly, monthly or annual installments, typically over a 3 to 5 year period.

Signs of Debt Trouble

- Your credit card balance is increasing.

- You only pay the minimum amount on credit card.

- You're using credit cards to pay for day-to-day living (groceries, petrol, food, etc).

- You have reached you maximum credit limit.

- You're working two jobs to pay debt.

- You don't pay using cash.

- Your savings account is diminishing.

Understanding the Importance of Credit Scores

We rely on credit to acquire the purchases we 'need' - from food and clothes to cars, education, travel, and a home. In order to qualify for credit, we have to prove to lending institutions that we can be relied upon to repay the debt when it becomes due, which means learning how to handle both your finances and credit carefully.

The first step towards being credit-wise is to learn about credit scores and how your credit worthiness is assessed by lending institutions. A credit score is a rating of creditworthiness that is based on credit reporting from lenders, such as banks, credit card companies, mortgage companies, landlords, utility companies, and other businesses that typically extend credit. These institutions submit reports to credit bureaus (such as Experian, TransUnion and Equifax) about you and your credit history. These credit bureaus, in turn, consolidate that information into a credit report that other lending institutions can access when assessing whether or not to advance new financial facilities to you or amend the terms of existing ones.

The credit report is a detailed history of your borrowing and repayment activities over a set number of years. It shows your current credit score, how much credit you have (credit lines), how much you currently owe, and how timely you make your payments. Quite often, lenders only report the people who are late and don't make note of the timely payers.

Your credit report will also reflect a value based on your debt-to-income ratio, which is the percentage of your total income that you owe in outstanding debt. Lenders often look for a debt-to-income ratio of less than 30 percent before they will lend. Before agreeing to extend credit, these lending institutions want to be sure that you aren't already too deeply in debt.

Credit Bureau Contact Details		
Experian Web: www.experian.com Tel: 888-397-3742	*TransUnion* Web: www.transunion.com Tel: 800-916-8800	*Equifax* Web: www.equifax.com Tel: 800-685-1111

How Credit Scores are Calculated

While credit bureaus use a number of different means to determine your credit rating, the most common means they employ is that of allocating a credit score. A credit score is simply an assessment, based on a scoring system, of your credit worthiness. The two systems most commonly used are the FICO and Vantage credit score systems. Basically, the higher you score, the better your credit rating. Details of the scoring systems are set out below.

FICO Credit Score Comparison

Score	Rating
730-850	Excellent
700-729	Great
670-699	Good
585-669	Average
300-584	Bad

Vantage Credit Score Comparison

Score	Rating
900-990	A
800-899	B
700-799	C
600-699	D
501-599	E

Important Tip

A bad or low credit score can affect you in a number of ways ranging from your ability to borrow, to enter into new rental agreements and even result in higher payments of interest rates and increased insurance premiums.

With two systems of assessment in operation, it can be quiet difficult for consumers to understand how they rate under each system – particularly where the top score available on the Vantage score system is 990 while, in comparison, the top score available on the FICO system is 850. To better understand how your score could translate from one system to another you could multiply your Vantage Score by 0.86 (850/990) to get an estimate of your FICO score. Similarly, you could multiply your FICO score by 1.16 (990/850) to get an approximate indication of your Vantage score.

If you don't already know your scores, you can visit the website www.myfico.com which will give you some guidance on how to calculate your credit rating. Similarly, if you visit http://www.bankrate.com/calculators/credit-score-fico-calculator.aspx, you will be taken step-by-step through a simple process to help you calculate your likely FICO score and rating.

What Happens to Your Credit Score When a Credit Application is Made?

Almost nothing escapes the view of the credit report. Every time you apply for a loan or credit line, the lender requests a copy of your credit report. When this happens, it's noted on your report as an "Inquiry". Whether you apply for a loan at a bank or in a store where a clerk asks you to apply for a store credit card, the credit bureau will know—and note it on your report. Inquiries remain on your credit report for two years. Ten percent of your total credit score is based on the number of credit applications you submit. Applying for a department store card can cost you up to 20 points on your score - which could signal the difference between loan approval and rejection.

Checking your own credit report will not impact your score, nor will accepting "pre-approved" credit card offers because those companies are not pulling your credit report and the credit bureau is therefore not alerted. The increase in your available credit, however, will be noted.

Reviewing Your Credit Report

As prospective lenders, landlords, and employers are likely to access your credit report from time to time, it's important to ensure that it's correct and accurate. To do this, you will need to review your report. You can get a free copy of your credit report once a year by visiting www.AnnualCreditReport.com. This is the only credit report source legally authorized by the Federal Trade Commission to provide this free service. However, you can also obtain a free copy of your credit report from other reputable sources such as www.credit.com. While many other companies may promote a 'free' credit report, some will charge a subscription fee or require you to purchase some other product or service before giving you access to your report. Be wary of these companies when requesting your report.

In addition to your entitlement to receive a free credit report annually, you are also entitled to request and receive a free report after you have been declined a loan or other form of credit. Where you have been so declined, the financial institution should send you written confirmation of the fact that your application for credit has been declined together with instructions on how you can receive a free copy of your credit report.

Once you get a copy of your report, the first thing you should do is ensure that the information in it is complete and accurate. Specifically, you should:

- Check your name, address, date of birth, and social security number – to ensure that it is in fact your credit report that the lending institution is viewing.

- Review all your outstanding debts and your payment history, including account numbers, total credit, and available credit. You might discover that someone else has been using your identity and racking up charges on credit cards that have unknown to you been issued in your name. You could also find other errors that need to be corrected.

- Check the "Last Activity" on each account to see how and when your payments were reported.

- Check the "Status" of each debt which will be coded as a combination of letters for the type of credit ("O" for "Open"; "R" for "Revolving"; and "I" for "Installment") and a number that rates your timeliness for many repayments. Low numbers (1 or 2) show that you pay on time or relatively close to the due date. Medium numbers (3 to 5) indicate late repayments between 60-120 days after the payments due date. Higher numbers (6 to 9) show you to be seriously behind on payments. High numbers indicate a potential forclosure or repossession may follow. It's essential that you ensure these records are accurate!

- Look to see if any accounts are listed as in collection. Delinquent bills that are turned over to a collection agency prompt a black mark on your credit report that can eliminate your chance of getting credit, so be sure this section is correct.

- Check the "Court Records" section which will show tax liens, bankruptcy, collection amounts, and any other judgments that are publicly recorded (such as delinquent child support payments in some states).

If you find errors in your credit report, contact the credit bureau that issued it. These reporting agencies are required by law to verify the accuracy of any information in your report within 30 days of receiving a written dispute letter from you. If the error remains, contact the lender who gave the information to the bureau and request that it notifies the bureau appropriately. It may take up to 45 days to have a dispute resolved if there is a mistake in your credit report. On the next page is a copy of a sample dispute letter provided by the Federal Trade Commission:

Sample Dispute Letter

Your Name
Your Address
City, State, Zip Code

Complaint Department
Name of Company
Address
City, State, Zip Code

Date

Dear Sir or Madam,

I am writing to dispute the following information in my file. I have circled the items I dispute on the attached copy of the report I received.

This item (identify item(s) disputed by name of source, such as creditors or tax court, and identify type of item, such as credit account, judgment, etc.) is (inaccurate or incomplete) because (describe what is inaccurate or incomplete and why). I am requesting that the item be removed (or request another specific change) to correct the information.

Enclosed are copies of (use this sentence if applicable and describe any enclosed documentation, such as payment records and court documents) supporting my position. Please reinvestigate this (these) matter(s) and (delete or correct) the disputed item(s) as soon as possible.

Sincerely,

[Your name]

Enclosures: (List what you are enclosing.)

How to Improve Your Credit Score

Now that you've learned the importance of having a good credit score, and hopefully checked out your credit report, you should take a few small steps to ensure that you either maintain or improve your existing score. To achieve this, you can use the following tips:

1. Pay your bills on time - not only will you avoid the expense of late fees, but you will also show that you responsibly manage your credit.

2. Reduce outstanding balances - pay down your balances before incurring new charges to keep your debt-to-income ratio at a reasonable level (below 30 percent).

3. Avoid having more than three credit card accounts at once - too much credit signals the potential to over-spend. However, don't close your credit card accounts either; this can in fact lower your score. Closing a credit card leaves you with less overall credit and instantly raises the percentage of your debt to credit ratio. Long standing credit history can help create a high credit score.

4. Use your credit cards and pay them regularly to show activity: Not using available credit can be as bad as over-using it. Lenders like to see activity on an account, which equates to purchases that are paid off on time.

5. Mix your credit types: A combination of timely payments on installment loans (mortgage, car, and student) with revolving credit cards shows you are a responsible credit user.

6. Review your credit report: Don't assume that all the information in your credit history is correct. Take advantage of the free annual credit report service and ensure that your reports are not compromised by errors.

Using credit wisely will help you achieve some personal goals without sacrificing your budget. Pay attention to your credit use (purchases and payments) so you can build the credit history that reflects the same commitment to responsibility that you will be demonstrate by living within your budget.

Personal Loans

Most commonly, individuals take out loans to buy a home or car, or finance a college education. But there are other times when we need to borrow money for emergency funds, like a medical bill, home repair, or even an unbudgeted (or under-budgeted) special event such as a wedding. Or we might just want to pay off high-interest debts to avoid the hefty finance charges. Personal or consumer loans might be the answer in these situations.

A personal loan allows an individual to borrow money that will be repaid over a specified period of time. Interest rates are often higher for personal loans than for other conventional loan programs, because they are viewed as riskier by lending institutions and are generally unsecured.

If you're considering a personal loan, you need to understand the different options available:

Secured loan:	This type of loan requires collateral, which means you need to put up property that equals or exceeds the value of the loan as security for that loan. If you default on the loan repayment, the lender may take your property and sell it to repay the loan.
Unsecured loan:	This loan requires no collateral but is based on your credit worthiness. Without collateral, however, the interest rates on unsecured loans are typically much higher than on secured loans.
Line of credit:	This option is like having a credit card. You are granted a specified limit of available credit and write a check against this account as needed. A line of credit is useful as a back-up resource, in case of emergency, but usually has an expiration or renewal date. At that time, the full balance must be paid off. This is similar to an overdraft facility.

Do You Need a Personal Loan?

There are advantages to securing a personal loan, like taking out a loan to consolidate debt and repay the balance at a lower interest rate. And there will be times when borrowing money seems like the best solution. Before choosing this route though, consider your options:

- Can your budget handle the repayment of the additional debt in a timely manner?

- How will the loan impact your credit?

- Will the additional loan expense change or affect your goals?

- Can you borrow the money from someone who will charge you little or no interest (e.g., family member or friend)?

If you decide that a personal loan is your best option, you can apply at your bank or to a variety of online lending sources. As with any loan, before you apply, check your credit report so you know what these lenders will be reviewing. Correct any errors. Then get quotes and terms (e.g., interest rate, monthly payment, length of loan, etc) from several lenders to ensure you get the best deal.

Paying Back Your Loan

Once you have decided to take out a loan, one of the most common questions you should ask about and understand is about repayments. Loans typically have three common components:

- Amount of the loan;

- Duration of the loan; and

- Interest rate charged.

To get an understanding of the impact of each, take the following loan comparison chart into consideration. It should give you some idea of how loans and credit ratings (which can lead to increased interest rates) can affect your budget. Note the impact of different interest rates and durations on the monthly repayment amount and the total cost of the loan.

Amount Borrowed	Duration of Loan	Interest Rate	Monthly Repayment	Total Cost of Loan	Interest Charged
3,000	3years	12% Fixed	104.08	3 747.14	747.14
6,000	3 years	8.3% Fixed	188.02	6,768.72	768.72
10,000	5 years	6.6% Fixed	195.23	11,713.80	1,713.80
25,000	10 Years	9% Fixed	535.61	32,136.56	7,136.56

Home Loans and Mortgages

As already mentioned, a home loan is very much like a personal loan except for the following key differences:

1. Home loans are usually advanced only for the purpose of buying a house or some other form of property.

2. The duration of home loans tend to be a lot longer than personal loans and can quite often be as long as 40 years. The duration of the loan makes it more affordable (in part) for the borrower as the repayment cost can be spread over a much longer period of time.

3. The interest rate is usually lower than standard personal loans. However, while it is lower, it should be remembered that with home loans much of the interest is paid back over the initial years of the loan. The consequence of this is that while you are making your repayments on your home loan, the principal amount of that loan (being the amount initially borrowed) is

only being paid off in a very small part in the initial years. The bulk of your initial repayments will be interest. The result is that it therefore takes a while before the principal amount of your loan begins to reduce.

4. Home loans are usually secured against the property that is purchased. As a result, if you fail to make your repayments when they are due, and this continues for a period of time, there is a real risk that you could lose your home.

When taking out a mortgage, shop around. The smallest difference in interest rates and duration can mean thousands of dollars on your overall mortgage cost. You will also need to understand how changes of interest rate can affect your monthly repayment amount and your ability to meet your repayments. Interest rates are discussed in brief in a later section.

Credit Cards and Common Misuses

Credit cards make it easy to purchase the products and services we want and need. When the bill arrives, sometimes a month after we've enjoyed the purchase, we're faced with the consequence of repaying the debt. To avoid getting into a difficult situation with your credit cards, *avoid* these common pitfalls:

Paying the minimum balance

The minimum payment required on credit cards is often little more than the interest accrued. If you can only manage to pay the minimum amount due, you will be paying the debt for a long time (see page 82 for further details). When making a credit card purchase, look at the actual value of the item or service you're buying. Add in the amount of time it will take to repay the debt plus the interest that will accrue during this time. When you add it up, is the purchase valuable enough to warrant the debt?

Getting too many cards

Don't collect credit cards like trading cards! Whether or not you use them, your numerous accounts will appear on your credit report and raise a red flag to possible lenders and employers. Try to have no more than three cards and use them and pay them off regularly.

Maxing out a card

When you use up your credit line, you demonstrate an uncontrolled spending habit, because you're spending more than you can efficiently repay. And you risk having the interest fees send you over your limit, which incurs over-limit fees and adds a black mark to your credit report.

Making late payments

Paying your credit card after the due date will add late charges and the tardiness appears on your credit report. A regular habit of late payments can also increase your interest rate on credit cards and loans, and decrease your credit line. To avoid late payments, set up an automatic payment schedule from your bank account.

Using the "Cash Advance" feature

A credit card is not a debit card. The fees that are charged for taking cash advances against your credit limit are expensive. You should avoid withdrawing cash on your credit card where possible.

Misunderstanding the introductory rate

When you receive offers of free financing or a low introductory rate, pay attention to the details. Quite often, the rate soars after a specified period. Unless you can repay the debt in the specified low to no-interest time period, calculate the cost of financing your expense at a considerably higher rate. Then decide if the offer is worthwhile.

Tips on Controlling Credit Card Costs

A few simple tips will help you keep within your budget:

- Keep track of your credit card spending.

- Remember that cash advances on a credit card can be expensive.

- Know your credit limit and do not exceed it – you might have to pay an additional fee if you do.

- Check your card statements carefully and tell your card issuer if you see any mistakes.

- Do not make purchases that you cannot afford to repay.

Are Balance Transfers on Credit Cards a Good Idea?

If you're carrying a balance on one credit card, it might be tempting to accept an offer from another for a zero percent annual percentage rate (APR). It's a good idea if you are transferring that amount to a card that currently has a zero balance. However, if you make the switch to a card where you already owe money, any monthly payment you make will go towards repaying the debt with the zero APR first and then remaining debt. As a consequence, the old or pre-existing debt will continue to accrue finance charges at the old rate on the card. Analyze the offer before committing to a balance transfer. Understand the costs involved. And be sure to adjust your budget accordingly.

How Much Credit is Necessary?

As stated in an earlier section, lenders will look at your credit report to see how much credit has been made available to you. If you have say $50,000 in available credit, a credit provider or lender that is considering extending credit or a loan to you could be concerned. Even if you're not using that credit line, it's available for use and you could use it. As such, if you chose to access it, the credit provider or lender will need to know that you will still be in a position to re-pay monies advanced by them in addition to the monies drawn under the new credit facility. Lenders may even insist in you closing some of those facilities before advancing you a loan.

Remember that credit is a financial privilege. You must use it responsibly in order to achieve your financial goals. Abusing credit by accepting every offer that is extended to you is a recipe for disaster. Not only will the available credit tempt you to overspend, but it could possibly prevent you from getting the mortgage or other loan that really matters.

Interest Rates

As you will have gathered from the above, an interest rate is the rate at which interest is paid by a borrower to a lender for the use of money that it has received from the lender. There are several different types of interest rates and it is important to understand some of the principal forms of interest rates. Two of the main rates are discussed below.

Fixed Rate

With a fixed interest rate, the rate of interest and repayment amount remains the same for the entire period of the loan, even when market interest rates fluctuate. So, for example, if you take out a personal loan for 3 years with a 7% fixed interest rate, that rate will not change during the loan period. Similarly, with a home loan, if you fix the interest rate at say 4.5% for the first 5 years then that rate will not change during that 5 year period. However, once the 5 year period is up, it can fluctuate in accordance with the rate charged by the lender.

While fixed interest rates can offer you the certainty of knowing what your repayments will be over a fixed period and protect you from interest rate increases, they also mean that you will not benefit from any interest rate cuts that occur during the fixed interest rate period. In addition, you may not be able to switch from the fixed rate to a variable rate easily.

Standard Variable Rate

With a standard variable rate of interest, your monthly repayments may rise and fall over the life of your loan depending on the rate of interest offered by the lender. While this means that you will be subject to the risk of interest rate rises, you will also have the advantage of being able to benefit from interest rate drops and being able to make early repayments on your loans.

Credit Card Repayments?

Have you ever considered just how much additional expense you are incurring by running up credit card debt and not paying it back promptly? In this section, we take a brief look at some of the different payment options available to credit cardholders, while also learning why it's better to discharge credit card debt sooner rather than later.

When it comes to credit cards, many of us pay only the minimum payment that is due each month. The result of doing so is that we end up repaying the debt for a prolonged period of time and, of course, continue to pay interest on the debt during that period. The net effect of this is that the costs of repaying the debt increase and we move further away from achieving our financial goals. To illustrate this, some examples are often helpful.

On page 84, three tables have been included to illustrate the different ways in which four credit cards debts of $3,000 can be repaid over a period of time. In Table A, only the minimum monthly repayment amount (as determined by the bank that issued the card) is repaid each month. In Tables B and C, a fixed amount determined by the cardholder is repaid each month. The interest rate (APR) varies for each card to illustrate the additional costs that cards with higher interest rates can incur.

Looking first at the data in Table A, the adverse effects of paying only the minimum balance each month become quickly apparent. It will take the cardholder between 93 to 109 months (that's between 7 to 9 years!) to fully repay his original $3,000 debt. During this time, interest charges of between $1,078.84 and $3,504.06 will be charged to him. If we look at the specific data for Card D, we can see that the amount of interest charged to the cardholder ends up being greater than the amount of the original debt. In other words, it cost him $3,504.06 in interest charges just to borrow $3,000. As a result, he ended up repaying $6,504.06. This very clearly illustrates the need to reduce the cost of credit card debt as quickly as possible. Of course, the only way of doing that is by repaying more than the bare minimum repayment amount each month.

In Tables B and C, the cardholder makes a fixed payment of $60 and $100 respectively each month to repay his credit card debt. These amounts are both in excess of the minimum monthly repayment amount that he needs to repay – and the benefits are immediately clear by comparison to the data in Table A. However, when we look more closely at the data in Tables B and C, we can also see the enhanced benefit obtained by making a larger repayment each month. If we look closely at the data for

Card A in both Table B and Table C, for example, we see two very different financial results. In the case of the $60 per month payment plan, the total interest charged is $1,031.45. This compares to a total charge of only $524.34 under the $100 per month fixed payment plan. This represents a total saving of $507.13 in total over the term of the debt. In addition, it takes 68 months to pay off the debt under the $60 per month payment plan compared with only 36 months (almost half the time) under the $100 per month plan. Now make the same comparisons for Card D under Tables B and C. In this case, a total saving of $2,061.21 is achieved while the debt is repaid 43 months earlier.

From the foregoing examples, the importance of repaying credit card debt as quickly as possible is clear to see. By doing so, not only will you benefit from significant cost savings but you will also repay the debt a lot sooner.

Determining Your Repayment Options

There are numerous online financial calculators and software available which will enable you to determine how best to reduce your credit card debt. By carefully reviewing your finances and formulating a suitable re-payment plan, you can reduce your credit card debt in an effective and intelligent manner. To help you formulate this plan, we have included a Credit Card Re-Payment Planner at the back of this book. This planner can be downloaded from our website www.enodare.com and full details on how you can do that are set out on page 17.

If you would like to look at some other helpful online resources in order to help you manage your credit card debt, some of flowing websites may be of benefit to you:

- **https://www.usbank.com/calculators/jsp/PayoffCC.jsp/**

- **http://www.bankrate.com/calculators/credit-cards/credit-card-payoff-calculator.aspx**

Table A - Paying The Minimum Balance on a Credit Card with a $3000 Balance

	Card A	Card B	Card C	Card D
Credit Card Balance	$3,000.00	$3,000.00	$3,000.00	$3,000.00
Annual Percentage Rate	11%	15%	19%	20%
Minimum Balance Calculated	3%	2.8%	2.2%	2.0%
Minimum Payment each Month	$90.00	$84.00	$66.00	$60.00
Months to Pay off Loan	93	114	81	109
Total Interest Paid	$1,078.84	$1,912.03	$2,343.63	$3,504.06
Total cost of Credit	$4,078.84	$4,912.03	$5,343.63	$6,504.06

Note: Banks may calculate the rates slightly different taking into consideration various circumtances.

Table B - Paying a $60 Fixed Monthly Payment on a Credit Card with a $3000 Balance

	Card A	Card B	Card C	Card D
Credit Card Balance	$3,000.00	$3,000.00	$3,000.00	$3,000.00
Annual Percentage Rate	11%	15%	19%	20%
Fixed Payment	$60.00	$60.00	$60.00	$60.00
Months to Pay off Loan	68	79	85	85
Total Interest Paid	$1,031.45	$1,737.36	$2,888.61	$3,254.71
Total cost of Credit	$4,031.45	$4,737.36	$5,888.61	$6,254.71

Note: Banks may calculate the rates slightly different taking into consideration various circumtances.

Table C - Paying a $100 Fixed Monthly Payment on a Credit Card with a $3000 Balance

	Card A	Card B	Card C	Card D
Credit Card Balance	$3,000.00	$3,000.00	$3,000.00	$3,000.00
Annual Percentage Rate	11%	15%	19%	20%
Fixed Payment	$100.00	$100.00	$100.00	$100.00
Months to Pay off Loan	36	38	42	42
Total Interest Paid	524.32	$783.57	$1,101.77	$1,193.50
Total cost of Credit	$3,524.32	$3,783.57	$4,101.77	$4,193.50
Additional Savings	$507.13	$953.79	$1,786.84	$2,061.21

Note: Banks may calculate the rates slightly different taking into consideration various circumtances.

CHAPTER 6

MAKING YOUR BUDGET PLAN

Chapter Overview

In this chapter, we'll help you prepare your budget based on your current income and expenditure levels, your financial goals and the cuts that you plan to make to your existing spending habits.

Getting Ready to Write Your Budget

Now that you have made a complete list of your incomes and expenditures and have a clear understanding of the financial goals that you want to achieve, it's time to prepare your budget. In preparing your budget, you will need to keep your financial goals at the forefront of your mind. Whether your goals are to make some savings or simply to pay off a credit card, it is these goals that will underpin your budget and keep you motivated to stick to it.

Like many budgets, your objective will be to maximize the uses to which you put your income by reducing your expenditures. Consider how much income you need to set aside from each paycheck to cover your expenses and meet your savings targets. Your savings goal must remain a priority and not be left to whatever remains when the bills are paid. Your goal with the budget is to create a stronger financial situation, not just live with your current one.

Determining Your Budget Figures

From Chapter 2, you now have a complete picture of your current income and expenditure levels. From Chapter 3, you have determined what financial goals you want to achieve from budgeting; and from Chapters 4 and 5you will have seen the many ways in which you can reduce your expenditure levels and will have hopefully implemented some of them. Now you need to bring all of this information and figures together into your budget.

Your budget will set out details of the money you have and how you intend to spend or save it over the next few months and years. It will be structured in a manner that is designed to help you achieve your financial goals.

Choosing Your Method of Budgeting

Discussed below are the two most common methods used in budgeting – the Envelope Method and the Spreadsheet Method – each of which was introduced in the first chapter. While both methods have their positives and negatives, if utilized properly each can be a very useful tool in enabling you to get up and running with your personal budget.

Once you have chosen your preferred method of budgeting, whether envelope or spreadsheet, you're ready to map out your financial blueprint.

Creating Your Budget Using the Envelope Method

The envelope method is a good way to ensure that you are actually setting aside money from your paycheck. With this method, you must physically put your cash into specific designated envelopes before spending any money on non-budgeted items. People who choose this approach to personal budgeting must be committed to making this "deposit" a first priority upon the receipt of each paycheck or incoming payment. This, however, is generally a short-term approach to budgeting rather than a long-term approach.

The first step in completing your budget is to review your current expenditure. As the envelope method involves a weekly budgeting process, you will need to review your weekly expenses carefully and decide where you can reduce those expenses. Remember to consider all of the appropriate cost reduction methods set out in Chapter 4. You should also consider the amount of money that you will need to set aside to meet your savings targets and other goals. You should at least try to reduce your expenses by a similar amount. Once you have decided where you can cut costs and the amount of each such cut, you will need to make careful note of each revised expenditure amount. When this is done, you will need to carry out the following steps:

1. Start by making an envelope for the money you want for your savings goal from each paycheck. Make this a priority. You'll never reach your goal unless you emphasize the importance of saving. You will hopefully have decided how much you want to save in the Goal Setting Worksheet.

2. Create the necessary envelopes for each expense category. You can use the categories listed in Chapter 3 or those listed on the spreadsheet or worksheet for guidance.

3. On each envelope, list the items and amounts that need to be included each week. This will be an amount based on your current revised expenditure levels.

4. Every week, you will need to set aside money into each envelope, regardless of whether the money is to meet a weekly or annual expense or saving. Write the amount that you have

determined you will need for each period:

(i)   For a monthly bill, divide the total amount by 4.3 to determine the weekly allotment. (Note: As there are 52 weeks in a year, you can't just divide your monthly payment by four. Using the figure of 4.3 gives you a much more accurate figure for a weekly breakdown.)

(ii)   Semi-annual bills should be divided by 26 to determine the weekly allowance.

(iii)   Annual bills should be divided by 52 to calculate the weekly amount to be put in the envelope.

(iv)   Using the figures you have for occasional and non-essential expenses, determine a weekly figure for each associated expense by calculating the total annual cost of all such expenses and dividing that figure by 52. You can take the necessary figures directly from your expense worksheets or budget spreadsheet.

Add up the total that you are placing into your envelopes each week to ensure that your expenses do not exceed your weekly income.

If your income isn't stretching as far as you need, you will either need to adjust your budget or employ some more of the expense reduction techniques in Chapter 4 to help it stretch a little bit further. You might even want to consider using the spreadsheet method, which provides a "big picture" perspective on income and expenses. It might be useful for you to see all of your costs laid side by side where you can compare, consider, and decide on any required changes.

Budgeting Should Be Fun!

Creating a budget is a trial and error process. In many ways, it's similar to using a recipe from a cookbook - it may take you a few attempts to get it just right! It's important to realize that budgeting, like diets, shouldn't just be about sacrifices and missing out. It should also include fun elements and things you like to do. When making your budget, you need to take into consideration fun elements such as clothing, entertainment, eating out and other things you like to do. Just because you are committed to a budget doesn't mean your life draws to a halt. So consider how you can reduce costs and continue to do the fun elements, just in moderation.

Creating Your Budget Using the Spreadsheet Method

The term "spreadsheet" might conjure up images of an accountant or some complicated mathematical formulae but, in fact, spreadsheets are relatively easy and straightforward to use. All you have to do is enter your figures into relevant boxes (called "cells") as indicated on the spreadsheet itself. It couldn't be easier. Once you enter these numbers, the spreadsheet program will automatically do the math for you.

The advantage of the spreadsheet method is that you can see your complete financial picture at a glance, rather than flipping through a stack of envelopes or worksheets. The accompanying budget spreadsheet also gives you clear snapshots of your financial situation using pie charts, graphs, tables and more.

In order to complete your spreadsheet budget, you will first need to review your current monthly expenditure levels. As part of this review, you will decide where you can cut some costs if you have not already done so using the Expense and Debt Reduction Worksheet from Chapter 4. It may be as obvious as giving up your morning trip to Starbucks. If it's not so obvious, take another look at the cost reduction suggestions set out in Chapter 4. Maybe you will find some suggestions there to guide you. The goal will be to reduce your current expenses by an amount at least equal to the amount you want to allocate towards your savings and towards meeting your financial goals.

Once you have decided where you can cut costs and the amount of each such cut, you will need to prepare your monthly budget. You will do this by clicking on the "Budget Forecast" tab in the Budget Spreadsheet. Once opened, you will need to enter details of your current income in the "Income" section at the top of the page. You should also enter details of your spouse's income if you are preparing a joint budget. However, if you are including your spouse's income you may need to include his or her expenses also and to make sure that he or she is 'on board' with the budgeting process.

Important Tip

If you wish to prepare a joint budget, you should ensure that each of the sections in the spreadsheet contains cumulative figures for you and your spouse.

The next step will be to enter the revised expenditure levels (whether for you alone or cumulatively for you and your spouse) for each category of expense. Take your time as this is where you really need to be honest and realistic about your budget plans. If you try to reduce your expenditure too much, your budgeting exercise will fail.

Once all the numbers are in place, go back and review them to make sure that they are correct. Compare the expense items listed in your budget with those listed in your monthly expenses to make sure you haven't missed any regular expenses.

If you are using the worksheets instead of the budget spreadsheet, then you can use the Monthly Expense Forecasting Worksheet to add the details of your revised spending goals - taking into account any planned reductions to your expenses that you plan to make.

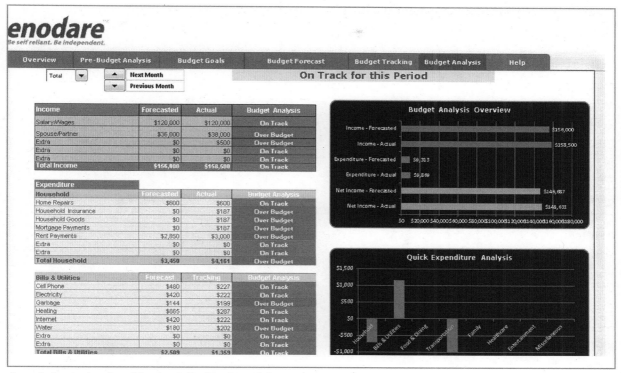

Sample Screenshot from Enodare's Budget Spreadsheet

Sample Budget Worksheet

The spreadsheet method of budgeting is one of the most important tools used in budgeting. For this reason, we have included at the end of this chapter a sample budget worksheet/spreadsheet to give you an understanding of how a completed budget should look. While it may appear at first glance to require a considerable effort to prepare a worksheet/spreadsheet like this, it is actually much easier that you might think. In fact, as you move slowly through each of the exercises in this kit, you will find yourself gathering and analyzing the information that you need in order to prepare a budget.

What to Do After Preparing Your Budget

Once you have prepared your budget, the next step will be to actually implement it. In order words, you will need to start living in accordance with the budget you have set for yourself and of course carefully monitor whether you are adhering to that budget. There are a number of items that you need to consider and take account of in order to do this. We'll discuss these in detail in the next chapter.

MONTHLY BUDGETING WORKSHEET					MONTH: September	
Start Date	Week 1 __/__/__	Week 2 __/__/__	Week 3 __/__/__	Week 4 __/__/__	Week5 __/__/__	Monthly _____
Income						
Salary/Wages	750	750	750	750		3000
Spouse/Partner	300	350	300	350		1300
Miscellaneous		150				150
Total Income	1050	1250	1050	1100		4450
Expenditure						
Household	260	300	250	250		1060
Bills & Utilities	120	65	30	150		365
Food & Dining	150	150	170	150		620
Transportation	125	100	115	95		435
Family	120	170	140	100		530
Healthcare		35				35
Entertainment	120	120	120	120		480
Miscellaneous	20	150	20	45		235
Savings	60	60	60	60		240
Total Expenditure	975	1150	905	970		4000
Total Surplus/Defecit	75	100	145	130		450

CHAPTER 7

LIVING WITH AND MAKING ADJUSTMENTS

TO YOUR BUDGET

Chapter Overview

Once the budget is established, you'll need to stick with it. Your financial success will be dependent on your ability to live within the financial plan you've created. This chapter will help you establish a way to be accountable for living within your budget and show you what to do when changes need to be made.

Creating Accountability

A budget is only going to work if you stick to the plan. Just as you would follow a doctor's medical advice, you should treat your personal budget as a prescription for your financial well-being. Skipping a "dose" by making a purchase you hadn't planned for or by postponing a deposit you planned to make to your savings account will only delay you in achieving your financial goals.

Preparing a budget is a big step and requires a lot of work. Living with that budget is an even bigger step. This plan will be your foundation for a long time—as long as it takes you to reach your goals, and perhaps beyond.

The best way to stick to a budget is to adopt a system that becomes a habit. A habit is the result of repeated behavior. By establishing a system to monitor your adherence to your budget, you create a system of checks and balances that keeps you accountable for your income and spending habits. Start by establishing a set of rules to follow regarding expenditures that allow you to stick to your budget plan. Force yourself into a habit of thinking before you spend. And at the end of every week, sit down and review your progress to determine how well you have stuck to your plan during that week.

Earlier, when discussing goals, we talked about setting short, medium and long-term objectives. These goals need to be written into your budget as a reminder of where this plan will take you. Create a set of weekly, monthly, quarterly, and annual goals, such as reducing your energy bills or entertainment expenses by a certain percent or reaching specific savings targets.

In the beginning, when enthusiasm is high, it will be an adventure to follow the budget and find ways to reduce expenses or increase income. Those initial successes coupled with your financial goals will provide you with the motivation to stay aligned with your budget. However, as you've committed to achieving certain goals, you will need to adhere to your budget until those goals are achieved. As such, you'll need to hold yourself accountable and remain keenly aware of how you're managing your finances.

How to Ensure You Stick to Your Budget

- Ensure your budget is reasonable and attainable

- Keep records of your spending

- Learn to negotiate spending by reducing costs and eliminating unnecessary expenses

- Make trade-offs where necessary

- Analyze your spending on a weekly and monthly basis

- Adjust your budget where necessary

- Create a reward system – budgeting doesn't mean you can't enjoy yourself or have fun!

Monitoring Your Progress

The only way you can prevent budgetary mishaps is by keeping an eye on how you're succeeding with your budget. Schedule a regular time each week when you can sit down and evaluate your progress. This should be a priority appointment with yourself, not a casual one that you easily postpone in favor of some other activity. Find the time when distractions are minimized and focus one hour on reviewing your budget. Put that appointment on your schedule as a weekly recurrence.

At the end of each week, update the "Daily Tracking Spreadsheet" spreadsheet by entering details of your receipts and expenses for the week just passed. This will ensure you have all the required information collected at the end of each month. If you are not using the spreadsheet, then use the Weekly Expense Tracking Worksheet to do this by entering details of your expenses for that same week. Compare the past week's outcome with your goals. Identify those areas where you have succeeded either in making savings or reducing spending and look for others where you incurred unexpected (e.g., car repair, medical tests, etc) or unbudgeted (e.g., impulse buys) expenses. Be aware of what prompted those additional expenses or any changes in income that you may have had. Did you over or under-estimate an item or simply run into an unexpected experience, like a job lay-off? Consider whether or not you need to adjust your budget to account for such outlays of cash in the future.

Remember - you must analyze all of your activities honestly in order to make the exercise worth your while. Did you really need to make each of the purchases you made? If so, did you actually need to spent the amount you spend it or could you have spent less?

When you review your budget progress each week, compare your anticipated and actual income and expenditure for that period and look for fluctuations - even minor ones can be significant as they can identity underlying spending habits or trends. Small shifts in spending habits could become much bigger problems if ignored. In fact, these shifts could also be an indication that you are sinking deeper into debt and that your budget or budgeting efforts are failing. Once you step outside the boundaries of your budget, even for a small expense, that one lapse could lead to others. Left unchecked, the budget will slowly disintegrate, along with the possibility of achieving the budget's goals.

Paying Attention to Your Spending

If you are using the budget spreadsheet, you should note that it contains two very useful tabs for helping you identify whether your actual monthly finances are on track with your budgeted monthly finances. These tabs are the "Budget Tracking" tab and the "Budget Analysis" tab. Each of these tabs was introduced in Chapter 1 and their value in monitoring and managing your finances should not be overlooked.

Making Adjustments to Your Budget

Your incomes and expenditures will change from time to time and so will your financial goals. As a result, you will need to update and adjust your budget to take account of these changes. Maybe these changes will come about because you've started a new job with better pay, or simply received a promotion, maybe it's because you've decided to get married and/or start a family or maybe your original goal was getting out of debt and, now that you have achieved that goal, you want to concentrate on creating savings. Perhaps your first budget was too conservative or too restrictive and you need to re-evaluate it. Whatever the reason for the need to change, you will need to think through the proposed changes to your budget carefully. The first thing that you will need to understand is why you are making that change to your budget -

- Did your income change?

- Were your estimations incorrect?

- Did you incur expenses you didn't expect?

- Did your expenses change in some way?

- Did you spend money on unbudgeted non-essentials items?

- Did your family size or situation change?

- Did you receive an inheritance or a windfall?

- Have your goals changed?

- Etc.

If any of these or other similar situations apply, how can you ensure your budget calculations will be more on target going forward? Do you need to update a particular aspect of your budget to take account of these new calculations? What other information do you need in order to more accurately predict your income and expenditure in the future? These are all questions which you must answer. Remember, it's essential that your budget is as comprehensive and precise as possible. Take the time to think carefully about budget changes before committing to making them. If you decide to make the change then be sure to either update your budget or, where circumstances require, create a new budget in its entirety. Remember, if your expenses increase you will need to find the money to meet those expenses from somewhere. It will be your job to determine where you can find that money and what cuts you may need to make to do so.

The Consequences of Budget Changes

Before making a budget adjustment, you should consider and ask yourself the following questions:

- **Is this a short-term change?**

   A budget adjustment doesn't have to be permanent. This change could be a temporary alteration to cover a bump in the road, like unemployment due to job loss or short-term disability from illness or injury. When a short-term adjustment is required, project a timeline for when you can return to your prior financial plan. Don't leave it open-ended. A goal without an action plan is merely a wish in disguise; goals are achievable, wishes are hopeful. Use the budget worksheets or budget spreadsheet to help you.

- **What will the shift in the budget do to your ability to pay your other bills?**

   When an unexpected expense arises, it's a natural reaction to panic. Stop and think about how one change in your budget will impact the rest of the flow. If you lower your monthly credit card payment to divert money elsewhere, you will be paying more finance charges, which increases your debt load? Is that change then worth the added expense and time added to your plan? Think carefully about the consequences of what you propose to do before acting.

- **Where can you cut spending?**

   Once you've created a balanced budget, where income meets expenses, you can't increase spending unless you also have an equal (or greater) increase in income. As such, some expense(s) will need to be cut in order to accommodate the spending change, so be clear about what you can sacrifice. This adjustment must be a shift you can live with or you will be revisiting your budget again.

- **Are you adjusting your goals, too?**

    Your budget was created to meet specific objectives based on your income and expense levels. If there is a change to either your level of income or your level of expenses, it may also impact how and when you achieve the goals. You might have less money to put in your savings, which means that buying the home, taking the vacation, or retiring early will be postponed. Ask yourself if that is an acceptable outcome before committing to the change. Otherwise, consider whether you can generate the extra money needed by making cuts elsewhere.

Ensuring Your Budget Helps Achieve Your Financial Goals

Your budget has been created in order to create a plan for the attainment of your financial goals. You are paving your way towards the attainment of these goals, week by week, by living within your budget. Change does happen. The best way to guarantee success with your budget and to reach those key milestones is to maintain a realistic budget, based on a lifestyle you can commit to living. No other person is going to benefit as much as you from the results of sticking to your budget. When friends encourage you to divert from your plan—to buy that expensive item or join them for a weekend away—remind them that you are focused on successfully achieving your goals and ask them to be supportive. When temptation occurs, consider the consequences. Is an incidental purchase worth delaying your dream?

Be completely honest with yourself when reviewing additional expenses and changes in your budget. Determine if it's really your budget or your mindset that needs a change.

Personal Finance Resources

Online Software	Mobile Application Software
• Mint.com (Intuit)	• Mint.com
• YNAB.com	• YNAB.com
• Finicity.com	• Wally
	• Goodbudget
Desktop Software	• Unsplurg
• Mint.com	
• Moneydance.com	

Conclusion

Budgeting is the art of financial discipline. It is possible to make savings and achieve your financial goals but it takes commitment, determination, motivation and, most importantly, the mental strength to follow through and make things happen. We all have these capabilities within us. It's simply a matter of invoking them when we need to. So dig deep, stay focused and let your budgeting take you where you want to be.......

To Your Budgeting Success!

WORKSHEETS

Appendix

WEEKLY EXPENSE TRACKING WORKSHEET

Overview

In order to understand where your weekly or monthly pay checks are going, you first need to understand where your money is going on a daily basis. This simple worksheet allows you to track your daily spending habits over the course of a week in order to give you an understanding of your weekly spending habits on each specific day of the week. The details that you accumulate during this period can be used to help you understand your more general spending habits.

The Worksheet

This worksheet contains expense columns for each of the 7 days of the week and then separate columns for details of your total weekly, monthly and annual expenses incurred during that period. The rows are divided up into a variety of expense categories reflecting some of the more common expenses that you might incur during a typical week.

How to Complete this Worksheet

Print off a copy of the Weekly Expense Tracking Worksheet and enter details of all of your expenditures over the course of a week. Include only those items that you pay for during this week long period. Do not include items that you pay for on a monthly or annual basis by attempting to divide them by 28/30/31 (monthly) or 365 (yearly), as the case may be, to get approximate daily figures. Doing this will give you a skewed vision of your weekly spending habits.

You need to capture each expense based on its frequency of payment. In this worksheet, we are looking at expenses that you typically incur over the course of a week such as lunch, travel, grocery and other similar expenses. If you make any payments during this week long period that are recurring monthly or annual payments, then make note of them in the "Monthly" or "Annual" columns so that they can be transferred to the relevant monthly and/or annual worksheets when you prepare them. You should not include any periodical expenses (other than daily or weekly expenses) in any of the seven day columns including, for example, monthly, quarterly or annual expenses. These expenses must be kept separate.

If you want to get a more detailed view of your spending habits, then once you have completed this worksheet, transfer the details to the Monthly Expense Forecast Worksheet.

Using the Budget Spreadsheet

If you plan on using the budget spreadsheet that accompanies this book then, at the end of the week, transfer details of all of your expenses into the "Current Spending" tab of the spreadsheet. Remember to carefully input the amount of each expense and select the frequency of that expense as either daily, monthly, yearly, etc.

WEEKLY EXPENSE TRACKING WORKSHEET								WEEK START_____		
Expenditure	Mon	Tue	Wed	Thurs	Fri	Sat	Sun	Weekly Total	Monthly	Annual
Household										
Home Repairs										
Household Goods										
Mortgage Payments										
Rent Payments										
Total										
Bills & Utilities										
Cell Phone										
Electricity										
Garbage										
Heating										
Internet										
Cable / TV										
Water										
Total										
Food & Dining										
Breakfast										
Dinner										
Groceries										
Lunch										
Take Away										
Tea/Coffee/Snacks										

WEEKLY EXPENSE TRACKING WORKSHEET								WEEK START_____		
Expenditure	Mon	Tue	Wed	Thurs	Fri	Sat	Sun	Weekly Total	Monthly	Annual
Total										
Transportation										
Car Loan Repayment										
Car Repairs										
Gas/Fuel										
Parking/Tolls										
Public Transport										
Registration										
Total										
Family										
Child Care										
Child Support										
Clothing										
Pet Expenses										
School Expenses										
Pocket Money										
Total										
Healthcare										
Dentist										
Doctor										
Eye care										
Medication										
Rehabilitation										

Weekly Expense Tracking Worksheet								Week Start		
Expenditure	Mon	Tue	Wed	Thurs	Fri	Sat	Sun	Weekly Total	Monthly	Annual
Total										
Entertainment										
Books & Magazines										
Events										
Movies & Theatre										
Music										
Travel										
Total										
Miscellaneous										
Clothing										
Donations										
Grooming										
Investments										
Loan										
Laundry/Dry Cleaning										
Bank Charges										
Savings										
Gifts										
Total										
Grand Total										

MONTHLY EXPENSE TRACKING WORKSHEET

Overview

This worksheet allows you to track your monthly spending habits in more detail by adding details of all items that you pay for during a given month. This worksheet is usually used in place of the Weekly Expense Tracking Worksheet. However, if you have already completed the weekly worksheet, you can transfer the data across as appropriate. Thereafter you can complete the details for the remaining days of the month. Once all of the required details have been added, you will have a detailed overall picture of your monthly spending habits. If you wish, you can transfer the totals from this worksheet to the Annual Expense Forecasting Worksheet to give you a better view of your annual spending habits.

The Worksheet

This worksheet contains expense columns for each of the 31 days of the month and then separate columns for details of annual or other periodical expenses incurred during the month long period. The worksheet also contains a number of rows which are divided up into a variety of different expense categories.

How to Complete this Worksheet

Start by printing off a copy of the Monthly Expense Tracking Worksheet. Once you've printed the worksheet, enter details of all of your expenditures over the course of a month. Do this on a daily basis. Do not include items that you pay for on a periodic basis greater than monthly (such as annually or biannually) and attempt to divide the figure to get an approximate daily/monthly figure. You need to capture each expense based on its frequency of payment!

Using the Budget Spreadsheet

If you are using the spreadsheet, you will simply need to enter details of the expenses incurred during the month and select the frequency of the payment for each expense. Remember to carefully input the amount of your spending and select the frequency of that spending.

If you make any payments during the month long period that are annual or non-monthly payments, then make note of them in the "periodical" or "Annual" columns so that they can be transferred to the relevant column of the Annual Expense Forecasting Worksheet when you prepare it. You should not include any periodical expenses (other than daily or weekly expenses) in any of the seven day columns including, for example, monthly, quarterly or annual expenses. These expenses must be kept separate.

MONTHLY EXPENSE TRACKING WORKSHEET		MONTH No:			START DATE:												
Expenditure Start Date	1	2	3	4	5	6	7	8	9	10	11	12	13	14	15	16	17
Household																	
Home Repairs																	
Household Goods																	
Mortgage Payments																	
Rent Payments																	
Total																	
Bills & Utilities																	
Cell Phone																	
Electricity																	
Garbage																	
Heating																	
Internet																	
Cable / TV																	
Water																	
Total																	
Food & Dining																	
Breakfast																	
Dinner																	
Groceries																	
Lunch																	
Take Away																	
Tea/Coffee/Snacks																	

Monthly Expense Tracking Worksheet Month No: Start Date: _____

Expenditure Start Date	1	2	3	4	5	6	7	8	9	10	11	12	13	14	15	16	17
Total																	
Transportation																	
Car Loan Repayment																	
Car Repairs																	
Gas/Fuel																	
Parking/Tolls																	
Public Transport																	
Registration																	
Total																	
Family																	
Child Care																	
Child Support																	
Clothing																	
Pet Expenses																	
School Expenses																	
Pocket Money																	
Total																	
Healthcare																	
Dentist																	
Doctor																	
Eye care																	

MONTHLY EXPENSE TRACKING WORKSHEET   MONTH NO: START DATE: _____

Expenditure Start Date	1	2	3	4	5	6	7	8	9	10	11	12	13	14	15	16	17
Medication																	
Rehabilitation																	
Total																	
Entertainment																	
Books & Magazines																	
Events																	
Movies & Theatre																	
Music																	
Travel																	
Total																	
Miscellaneous																	
Clothing																	
Donations																	
Grooming																	
Investments																	
Loan																	
Laundry/Cleaning																	
Bank Charges																	
Savings																	
Gifts																	
Total																	
Grand Total																	

MONTHLY EXPENSE TRACKING WORKSHEET								MONTH NO:		START DATE:					
Expenditure Start Date	18	19	20	21	22	23	24	25	26	27	28	29	30	31	**Periodically**	**Annual**
Household																
Home Repairs																
Household Goods																
Mortgage Payments																
Rent Payments																
Total																
Bills & Utilities																
Cell Phone																
Electricity																
Garbage																
Heating																
Internet																
Cable / TV																
Water																
Total																
Food & Dining																
Breakfast																
Dinner																
Groceries																
Lunch																
Take Away																
Tea/Coffee/Snacks																
Total																

MONTHLY EXPENSE TRACKING WORKSHEET MONTH NO: START DATE: _____

Expenditure Start Date	18	19	20	21	22	23	24	25	26	27	28	29	30	31	Periodically	Annual
Transportation																
Car Loan Repayment																
Car Repairs																
Gas/Fuel																
Parking/Tolls																
Public Transport																
Registration																
Total																
Family																
Child Care																
Child Support																
Clothing																
Pet Expenses																
School Expenses																
Pocket Money																
Total																
Healthcare																
Dentist																
Doctor																
Eye care																
Medication																
Rehabilitation																

MONTHLY EXPENSE TRACKING WORKSHEET							MONTH No:		START DATE:						
Expenditure Start Date	18	19	20	21	22	23	24	25	26	27	28	29	30	31	Periodically	Annual
Total																
Entertainment																
Books & Magazines																
Events																
Movies & Theatre																
Music																
Travel																
Total																
Miscellaneous																
Clothing																
Donations																
Grooming																
Investments																
Loan																
Laundry/Cleaning																
Bank Charges																
Savings																
Gifts																
Total																
Grand Total																

MONTHLY EXPENSE FORECASTING WORKSHEET

Overview

This worksheet supplements the Weekly Expense Tracking Worksheet by allowing you to forecast your likely spending habits over the course of a given month. To create your forecast, you will add details of your estimated daily expenditure for each of the first 4 weeks of the month. These estimates will be based on the expense details accumulated during your week long expense tracking exercise. Once you have done this, you will use the same Weekly Expense Tracking Worksheet to include an estimated amount for the remaining days of the month. Thereafter, you will add details of any monthly payments recorded in your Weekly Expense Tracking Worksheet and, finally, any monthly expenses that may not have already been recorded in that worksheet. For example, suppose you pay your rent at the end of each month, but the Weekly Expense Tracking Worksheet was prepared in respect of the first week of the month. In that case, as your rent will not have been included in the monthly column of the Weekly Expense Tracking Worksheet, you will need to add details of that expense and indeed any other monthly expenses in the Monthly Expense Forecasting Worksheet.

The Worksheet

This worksheet contains an expense column for each of the 4 ½ weeks that fall during a calendar month, a column for total monthly expenses and, finally, a column for annual and periodical expenses. It also contains a number of rows which are divided up into a variety of expense categories reflecting some of the more commonly incurred expenses.

How to Complete this Worksheet

Print off a copy of the Monthly Expense Forecasting Worksheet and enter details of your average weekly expenses (which will appear in the total column of the Weekly Expense Tracking Worksheet) in the columns for weeks 1 to 4. As week 5 will consist of only part of the week, you should calculate this figure based on the daily figures taken in your Weekly Expense Tracking Worksheet. For example, if you know that there are 31 days in this month and the final 3 days (31 days less the 28 days already included in the columns for weeks 1 to 4) will be Thursday, Friday and Saturday, you can take the totals for each of these three days from your Weekly Expense Tracking Worksheet, add them together and then place the total under Week 5. This will give you a clearer picture of your spending in that month.

If you listed any monthly expenses in the Weekly Expense Tracking Worksheet, transfer those totals to the "Monthly Expenses" column of this worksheet. In addition, you should also add details of any other monthly expenses which have not already been included in the worksheet in to this column.

As before, do not include items that you pay for on an annual basis and attempt to divide them by 52 or 12 to get an approximate weekly or monthly value.

If you want to get a more detailed view of your spending habits, transfer the details from your Monthly Expense forecasting Worksheet to the Annual Expense Forecasting Worksheet.

Using the Budget Spreadsheet

If you plan on using the budget spreadsheet that accompanies this book then, at the end of the month, transfer details of all expenses not already included in the spreadsheet (which will be the new monthly figures that you added) into the "Current Spending" tab of the spreadsheet. Remember to carefully input the amount of each expense and select the frequency of that expense. Do not duplicate any expenses that you may have already added when transferring your balances from the Weekly Expense Tracking Worksheet.

MONTHLY EXPENSE FORECASTING WORKSHEET

Expenditure Start Date	Week 1 __/__/__	Week 2 __/__/__	Week 3 __/__/__	Week 4 __/__/__	Week5 __/__/__	Monthly	Annual
Household							
Home Repairs							
Household Goods							
Mortgage Payments							
Rent Payments							
Total							
Bills & Utilities							
Cell Phone							
Electricity							
Garbage							
Heating							
Internet							
Cable / TV							
Water							
Total							
Food & Dining							
Breakfast							
Dinner							
Groceries							
Lunch							
Take Away							
Tea/Coffee/Snacks							
Total							

MONTHLY EXPENSE FORECASTING WORKSHEET

Expenditure Start Date	Week 1 __/__/__	Week 2 __/__/__	Week 3 __/__/__	Week 4 __/__/__	Week5 __/__/__	Monthly	Annual
Transportation							
Car Loan Repayment							
Car Repairs							
Gas/Fuel							
Parking/Tolls							
Public Transport							
Registration							
Total							
Family							
Activities							
Child Care							
Child Support							
Clothing							
Pet Expenses							
School Expenses							
Pocket Money							
Total							
Healthcare							
Dentist							
Doctor							
Eye care							
Medication							
Rehabilitation							

MONTHLY EXPENSE FORECASTING WORKSHEET

Expenditure Start Date	Week 1 __/__/__	Week 2 __/__/__	Week 3 __/__/__	Week 4 __/__/__	Week5 __/__/__	Monthly	Annual
Total							
Entertainment							
Books & Magazines							
Events							
Movies & Theatre							
Music							
Travel							
Total							
Miscellaneous							
Clothing							
Donations							
Grooming							
Investments							
Loan							
Laundry/Cleaning							
Bank Charges							
Savings							
Gifts							
Total							
Grand Total							

ANNUAL EXPENSE FORECASTING WORKSHEET

Overview

This worksheet supplements the Monthly Expense Tracking Worksheet and the Monthly Expense Forecasting Worksheet by allowing you to forecast your likely spending habits over the course of a given year. To create your forecast, you will add details of your actual or, as the case may be, forecasted monthly expenditure for each of the 12 months of the year. Once you have done this, you will add details of any annual payments recorded in your Weekly Expense Tracking Worksheet or Monthly Expense Tracking Worksheet as well as any annual or other periodical expenses that may not have already been recorded in the other worksheets.

The Worksheet

This worksheet contains an expense column for each of the 12 months of the year, a column for other annual expenses and a column for total annual expenses. It also contains a number of rows which are divided up into a variety of expense categories reflecting some of the more commonly incurred expenses.

How to Complete this Worksheet

Print off a copy of the Annual Expense Forecasting Worksheet and enter details of your average monthly expenses (which will appear in the total column of the Monthly Expense Tracking Worksheet or, as the case may be, Monthly Expense Tracking Worksheet) in the columns for each of the 12 months of the year. If you listed any annual expenses in either your Weekly Expense Tracking Worksheet or your Monthly Expense Tracking Worksheet, transfer those totals to the "Annual Expenses" column of this worksheet. In addition, you should also add details of any other periodical expenses that many not have already been included in the worksheet in to this column.

Using the Budget Spreadsheet

If you plan on using the budget spreadsheet that accompanies this book, then transfer details of all expenses not already included in the spreadsheet (which will be the new annual and periodical figures that you added) into the "Current Spending" tab of the spreadsheet. Remember to carefully input the amount of each expense and select the frequency of that expense. Do not duplicate any expenses that you may have already added when transferring your balances from other worksheets.

Important Note Regarding Annual Expenses

if you have calculated your monthly expenses using 31 days, this will represent a total of 372 days (31*12) in your annual expense forecast!

As such, to give you a fairer representation of the actual expenses, you should deduct 1 full weeks expense from the total (372-7 =365).

ANNUAL EXPENSE FORECASTING WORKSHEET
START _____

Expenditure	Jan	Feb	Mar	Apr	May	Jun	Jul	Aug	Sep	Oct	Nov	Dec	Total	Other Annual Expenses
Household														
Home Repairs														
Household Insurance														
Household Goods														
Mortgage Payments														
Rent Payments														
Total														
Bills & Utilities														
Cell Phone														
Electricity														
Garbage														
Heating														
Internet														
Cable / TV														
Water														
Total														
Food & Dining														
Breakfast														
Dinner														
Groceries														
Lunch														
Take Away														
Tea/Coffee/Snacks														
Beverages														

ANNUAL EXPENSE FORECASTING WORKSHEET
START_____

Expenditure	Jan	Feb	Mar	Apr	May	Jun	Jul	Aug	Sep	Oct	Nov	Dec	Total	Other Annual Expenses
Total														
Transportation														
Car Insurance														
Car Loan Repayment														
Car Repairs														
Gas/Fuel														
Parking/Tolls														
Public Transport														
Registration														
Total														
Family														
Child Care														
Child Support														
Clothing														
Pet Expenses														
Pet Insurance														
School Expenses														
Tuition Fees														
Pocket Money														
Total														
Healthcare														
Dentist														
Doctor														
Eye care														

ANNUAL EXPENSE FORECASTING WORKSHEET
START_____

Expenditure	Jan	Feb	Mar	Apr	May	Jun	Jul	Aug	Sep	Oct	Nov	Dec	Total	Other Annual Expenses
Health Insurance														
Medication														
Rehabilitation														
Total														

Books & Magazines														
Events														
Memberships														
Movies & Theatre														
Music														
Subscriptions														
Travel														
Total														

Miscellaneous														
Clothing														
Donations														
Grooming														
Investments														
Loan														
Laundry/Cleaning														
Bank Charges														
Savings														
Gifts														
Total														

Grand Total														

GOAL SETTING WORKSHEET

Overview

To make your goals become a reality, you need to write them down and, of course, take actions to achieve them. The two worksheets below allow you to enter a goal, the duration in which you expect to achieve that goal, whether that goal is a high, medium or low priority and the actions that you need to take in order to attain that goal.

The Worksheets

There are two separate goal setting worksheets in this section. One is for short term goals and the other is for longer term goals. Each worksheet contains a number of specific columns which require you to consider the importance of each goal, what you need to do in order to achieve that goal and when. These columns allow you to identify your specific goals and include important information about each of those goals including the priority of the goals, start dates, finish dates, costs involved, Actions and motivational factors required to achieve those goals.

How to Complete this Worksheet

Complete your worksheet using the following steps:

1. Identify each of your financial goals and write them down in the "Goal" column. Be as clear and descriptive about each of your goals as possible. Don't simply write down "to buy a new car". Write down the make, model, color and any other pertinent details of the car you want. Do this for all of your goals and spend time at it. Research has consistently shown that by being as clear and detailed as possible in describing your goals, you dramatically increase the probability of attaining them.

2. Specify how long you expect it to take to achieve each of your goals. You may need to work backwards on some of these. For example, if you know the cost of achieving your goal is $5,000 and that you can only contribute $100 a month towards reaching this target, you will need 50 months, or 4 years and two months, to accomplish that goal. It is a good idea to specify start and finish dates as well as the duration, this will enable you to monitor your progress at a later stage.

3. Decide on a priority level for each of your goals. Use the following priority indicators:-

   #1   =   "High" or "Very important".

   #2   =   "Medium" or "Fairly important".

#3   =   "Low" or "Not very important".

#4   =   "None" or "Not important". Items falling in this category are really items that you would like to have but are not that important in the bigger scheme of things such as, for example, a new outfit for the party next weekend.

By attributing a priority level to each item, you can quickly decide which goals you might want to forsake if your budget hits a 'bump on the road". Alternatively, you can determine

which goals to focus on if your current financial position doesn't allow you to pursue all of them at once.

4.   In the fourth column, insert the financial amount that the goal will cost to achieve. In addition to setting out the total cost, break this figure down into a monthly amount so that you can allocate an appropriate amount in your monthly budget (which you will prepare later) to meet this cost. Be realistic in identifying how much you can allocate. It may not be possible to achieve all of your goals at once. You should add up the monthly cost of all of your goals so that you can determine whether it is compatible with your overall budget. Remember, that if you are setting aside an amount on a monthly basis to achieve these goals, that amount needs to feature in your budget and, more importantly, your budget must have sufficient scope financially to allow for it!!! If not, you may need to forego a goal for now (this is where priority allocation comes in) or adjust the timeframe for achieving it and the monthly amount required to do so.

5.   A goal is of little value unless you can actually achieve it!! In the "Actions" column set out the specific things that you will do to help meet the cost of achieving each goal. There may be a specific sacrifice that you are willing to make in order to achieve a specific goal or indeed several goals. At the end of the day, you will need to make enough financial sacrifices and/or cut-backs as are necessary to achieve your goals and you will need to know how to do that. If you cannot do this, the unfortunate reality is that some or all of your goals are simply not realistic. Remember goals can only be achieved if they are realistic!

6.   IIn order to keep you motivated towards achieving each goal, you should clearly set out motivational factors why you want to achieve each particular goal. How will you benefit from achieving a particular goal? How will you feel? What are the advantages? Add as many reasons as you can. Again, research has shown that by clearly knowing why you want to achieve a particular goal, you will remain more focused on it and more likely to achieve it.

GOAL SETTING WORKSHEET - SHORT TERM

In order to make your goals become a reality, you must write them down. The worksheet below allows you to enter your goals, the duration in which you expect to achieve each goal, whether the goal is a high, medium or low priority and the actions that you need to take in order to attain your goals.

Goal	Duration	Priority	Annual and Monthly Goal Cost	Actions	Motivational Factors

GOAL SETTING WORKSHEET - LONG TERM

In order to make your goals become a reality, you must write them down. The worksheet below allows you to enter your goals, the duration in which you expect to achieve each goal, whether the goal is a high, medium or low priority and the actions that you need to take in order to attain your goals.

Goal	Duration	Priority	Annual and Monthly Goal Cost	Actions	Motivational Factors

EXPENSE AND DEBT REDUCTION WORKSHEET

Overview

One of the most important exercises in budgeting is actually reducing the expenses that you incur on a daily, weekly, monthly and annual basis. You will already have details of these expenses in your various expense worksheets. The Expense and Debt Reduction Worksheet allows you to highlight specific expenses and debts and set out methods by which you can reduce them. You can then track your progress by monitoring whether the related "key actions" have been followed through or not.

The Worksheet

The worksheet is divided into a number of columns and rows which allow you to enter details in respect of the debt/expense you want to reduce, the method by which you are going to do that and the key steps or actions involved in implementing that method. The final column, the "action completed" column, allows you to track your progress by checking the boxes located opposite each key action point.

How to Complete this Worksheet

Completing the worksheet is very straightforward. Simply enter details of the debt or expense you want to reduce and how you plan to do it. You should refer to Chapter 4 for details of a variety of different means by which you can reduce your debts and expenses.

EXPENSE AND DEBT REDUCTION WORKSHEET

Expense/ Debt	Method(s) of Reduction	Key Action Points	Action Completed
			☐ ☐ ☐ ☐
			☐ ☐ ☐ ☐
			☐ ☐ ☐ ☐
			☐ ☐ ☐ ☐
			☐ ☐ ☐ ☐
			☐ ☐ ☐ ☐
			☐ ☐ ☐ ☐
			☐ ☐ ☐ ☐
			☐ ☐ ☐ ☐
			☐ ☐ ☐ ☐
			☐ ☐ ☐ ☐
			☐ ☐ ☐ ☐

LOAN AND DEBT REPAYMENT PLANNER

Overview

The first step in getting out of debt or simply paying off a particular debt is understanding that debt – to whom it's owed, is current repayment obligations, the rate of interest payable and the term of the debt. You should be able to find out the relevant information by digging out your most recent statements for the debt in question. These debts can include car loans, student loans, home equity loans, personal loans, car loans, appliance loans, loans from friends and family and any other type of debt that you might have from time to time. We have included a separate repayment planner for credit card debt so you should use that planner for setting out your repayment plans for your credit card(s).

The Worksheet

The worksheet contains an information section at the top of the page which allows you to input certain information regarding the debt such as details of the creditor to whom the debt is owed, the account number, the balance due and the interest rate. You should insert these details so that you have them to hand if you want to compare the cost of that particular debt against another. Below the information section, the worksheet is divided into a number of columns (one for each month of the year) and rows. The row headings include:

-   "Starting Balance" - When you first start using the payment planner, the starting balance will be that as shown on your most recent account statement. After that, however, the balance used at the start of each month will be the estimated closing balance from the previous month having taken into account details of any repayments made and any interest charged, in each case, during that previous month.

-   "Payment" – This is the actual or estimated amount of any repayments made or to be made during a particular month.

-   "Interest Charge" – Each month interest will be payable on any balance due on the debt. You will need to calculate this amount based on the applicable interest rate.

-   "Closing Balance" - This will be the end balance for each month and, in turn, the opening balance for the next month.

How to Complete this Worksheet

To complete the worksheet, the first thing that you will need to do is obtain a copy of your most recent account statement for the relevant debt. This will provide you with the details to be inserted into the information section of the worksheet as well as the balance owing on your particular account. Once you have got your statement, print off a copy of the worksheet. Now, add the relevant details in the information section as well as the opening balance in the month in which you are stating your payment plan. The next step will be to insert an amount for monthly repayments. This may either be the set amount that you are required to pay each month or perhaps a higher amount that you chose to pay in order to get the debt paid off quicker. You will need to give careful consideration to the amount that you will be able to pay each month. Finally, the interest amount payable per month will depend on the interest rate as well as the closing balance on the account at the end of each month. Remember, the amount of interest payable each month should be reducing from month to month – unless the interest rate is fixed for the term of the debt.

LOAN AND DEBT REPAYMENT PLANNER

Loan/Debt Details: _____

_____

Creditor Name:	_____	**Amount Owed:**	_____
Account No:	_____	**Interest Rate:**	_____
Telephone No:	_____		

	Jan	Feb	Mar	Apr	May	Jun	Jul	Aug	Sep	Oct	Nov	Dec	Total
Starting Balance													
Payment													
Interest Charge													
Closing Balance													

LOAN AND DEBT REPAYMENT PLANNER

Loan/Debt Details: _____

_____

Creditor Name:	_____	**Amount Owed:**	_____
Account No:	_____	**Interest Rate:**	_____
Telephone No:	_____		

	Jan	Feb	Mar	Apr	May	Jun	Jul	Aug	Sep	Oct	Nov	Dec	Total
Starting Balance													
Payment													
Interest Charge													
Closing Balance													

LOAN AND DEBT REPAYMENT PLANNER

Loan/Debt Details: _____
_____

Creditor Name:						**Amount Owed:**								
Account No:						**Interest Rate:**								
Telephone No:														
	Jan	**Feb**	**Mar**	**Apr**	**May**	**Jun**	**Jul**	**Aug**	**Sep**	**Oct**	**Nov**	**Dec**	**Total**	
Starting Balance														
Payment														
Interest Charge														
Closing Balance														

LOAN AND DEBT REPAYMENT PLANNER

Loan/Debt Details: _____
_____

Creditor Name:						**Amount Owed:**								
Account No:						**Interest Rate:**								
Telephone No:														
	Jan	**Feb**	**Mar**	**Apr**	**May**	**Jun**	**Jul**	**Aug**	**Sep**	**Oct**	**Nov**	**Dec**	**Total**	
Starting Balance														
Payment														
Interest Charge														
Closing Balance														

CREDIT CARD REPAYMENT PLANNER

Overview

Due to the high rate of interest charged on credit cards, credit card debt is one of the biggest contributors to bankruptcy in the United States. For this reason, the repayment of credit card debt should often take priority over the repayment of most other debts as those debts will typically carry lower interest rates. Our Credit Card Repayment Planner will help you work out a repayment plan for your credit card. If you have more than one card, you should aim to pay off the card with the highest annual percentage rate of interest (APR) first as this card will be costing the most on interest payments. For each credit card you have, you should prepare a separate Credit Card Repayment Planner worksheet as this will allow you to more precisely plan your repayments. Of course, the repayments all need to fit into your overall budget.

The Worksheet

The worksheet contains an information section at the top of the page which allows you to input certain information regarding the credit card debt such as details of the credit card company to whom the debt is owed, account number, balance due and APR.. You should insert these details so that you have details of the account to hand. Below the information section, the worksheet is divided into a number of columns (one for each month of the year) and rows. The row headings include:

- "Starting Balance" - When you first start using the payment planner, the starting balance will be the date on your most recent credit card statement. After that, however, it will be the estimated closing balance from the previous month having taken into account details of any new transactions made, any repayments made and any interest charged, in each case, during that previous month.

- "Purchases" – This is the amount of any actual or estimated purchases made during each month. Obviously, you should try to keep purchases to a minimum during any period in which you are trying to pay off a credit card.

- "Repayments" – This is the actual or estimated amount of any repayments made during the month.

- "Interest Charge" – Each month interest will be payable on any balance due on the credit card.

- "Closing Balance" - This will be the end balance for each month and, in turn, the opening balance for the next month.

How to Complete this Worksheet

To complete the worksheet, the first thing that you will need to do is obtain a copy of your most recent credit card statement. This will provide you with the details to be inserted into the information section of the worksheet as well as the balance owing on your credit card. Once you have got your statement, print off a copy of the worksheet. Now, add the relevant details in the information section as well as the opening balance in the month in which you are starting your payment plan. The next step is to enter an amount for the credit card purchases you will make during each month, an amount for each monthly repayment that you will make and an amount for the interest payable each month. If you do not plan on using your credit card or, alternatively, limiting your monthly credit card expenses to a specific amount you should be able to insert a specific figure in the Purchases column – even if that figure is zero. The next step will be to insert an amount for monthly repayments. This may be a set amount per month or may vary from month to month. You will need to give careful consideration to the amount that you will be able to pay each month. Finally, the interest amount payable per month will depend on the annual percentage rate of interest payable on your credit card and the balance owing on your account on each monthly interest date. You will need to make a rough estimate of this figure based on the closing balance each month. Remember, the amount of interest payable each month should be reducing from month to month if you are repaying more than you are spending on your card.

Determining Your Repayment Options

There are numerous online financial calculators and software available which will enable you to determine how best to reduce your credit card debt. By carefully reviewing you finance and determining a suitable payment plan, you can reduce your credit card debt and move closer to becoming debt free. Listed below are several websites offering such services as well as a Debt Calculator spreadsheet which is available with this kit.

A copy of the Debt Calculator Spreadsheet can be downloaded from enodare.com (see page 17 for details).

- http://www.federalreserve.gov/creditcardcalculator/

- http://www.bankrate.com/calculators/credit-cards/credit-card-payoff-calculator.aspx

- http://www.thecalculatorsite.com/finance/calculators/credit-card-payment-calculators.php

CREDIT CARD REPAYMENT PLANNER

Credit Card Details: _____

_____

Creditor Name: _____ **Amount Owed:** _____

Account No: _____ **Interest Rate:** _____

Telephone No: _____

	Jan	Feb	Mar	Apr	May	Jun	Jul	Aug	Sep	Oct	Nov	Dec	Total
Starting Balance													
Purchases													
Repayments													
Interest Charge													
Closing Balance													

CREDIT CARD REPAYMENT PLANNER

Credit Card Details: _____

_____

Creditor Name: _____ **Amount Owed:** _____

Account No: _____ **Interest Rate:** _____

Telephone No: _____

	Jan	Feb	Mar	Apr	May	Jun	Jul	Aug	Sep	Oct	Nov	Dec	Total
Starting Balance													
Purchases													
Repayments													
Interest Charge													
Closing Balance													

CREDIT CARD REPAYMENT PLANNER

Credit Card Details: _____

_____

Creditor Name:	_____	**Amount Owed:**	_____
Account No:	_____	**Interest Rate:**	_____
Telephone No:	_____		

	Jan	Feb	Mar	Apr	May	Jun	Jul	Aug	Sep	Oct	Nov	Dec	Total
Starting Balance													
Purchases													
Repayments													
Interest Charge													
Closing Balance													

CREDIT CARD REPAYMENT PLANNER

Credit Card Details: _____

_____

Creditor Name:	_____	**Amount Owed:**	_____
Account No:	_____	**Interest Rate:**	_____
Telephone No:	_____		

	Jan	Feb	Mar	Apr	May	Jun	Jul	Aug	Sep	Oct	Nov	Dec	Total
Starting Balance													
Purchases													
Repayments													
Interest Charge													
Closing Balance													

GIFT GIVING WORKSHEET

Overview

The cost of making gifts can often be one of the most frequently overlooked expenses incurred in a given financial year. Just consider the significant costs incurred in making gifts on events such as birthdays, anniversaries, Christmas and other religious holidays, weddings, father/mother's day, graduations, Valentine's Day and so on. The problem is of course compounded when you consider the amount of people to whom you may have to make such gifts – children, parents, siblings and other family members; not to mention friends, children's friends, neighbours, co-workers and more. If you don't keep a careful watch on your spending habits you could easily see the cost of annual gift giving reach hundreds or even thousands of dollars. This worksheet is designed to help you make a longer term forecast of the gifts that you will need to make over a particular period, allocate a budget to those gifts and then monitor your spending as and when you make each of your purchases.

The Worksheet

The worksheet will allow you to insert details of all of the gifts that you plan to make over a period of time. It contains the following columns:

- "Name" – The name of each of your proposed beneficiaries;

- "Relationship" - The relationship between you and each proposed beneficiary;

- "Occasion" - The occasion for which the gift is being purchased. This could be an occasion like a birthday, a wedding, a baby shower, etc.

- "Month Due" - Enter the date and month in which you will need to buy the gift.

- "Gift " – Enter the details of the gift required.

- "Payment Method" – The method (such as cash or credit card) you plan on using to make your purchase. If you are using cash, you may even want to specify whether you intend to use savings, wages or other money due to you to make the payment when the time comes.

- "Budgeted Cost" – The budgeted amount for your gift.

- "Actual Cost" - The actual cost of your gift.

- "Variance" - The difference between the Budgeted Cost and Actual Cost. If you have spent less than the budgeted amount for the gift then insert -$[amount]. If you have spent more, insert +$[amount]. If you have spent more or less than planned you may wish to adjust the amount you have budgeted for other gifts so that you can ensure that you keep to your budget amount for gifts generally.

How to Complete this Worksheet

Completing this worksheet is the easy part.....deciding on gift ideas that fall within your budget can be a little more challenging! To complete the worksheet, either print off a copy or save a copy to your computer. Next, simply start inputting the details required in each column. This should be very straightforward. You will need to carefully consider the amount that you can budget for the gift in question. To get the real benefit from this exercise, however, it's a good idea to plan ahead for a few months documenting details of all the gifts you will need to make during that period. This will enable you take more of a 'global view' when deciding how much to allocate for each specific gift. Hopefully, by seeing the sum total of your proposed spending for the period, it will lead you to make more considered decisions about the amount that you will spend on each individual gift.

GIFT GIVING WORKSHEET

Name	Relationship	Occasion	Month Due	Gift	Payment Method	Budgeted Cost	Actual Cost	Variance

GIFT GIVING WORKSHEET

Name	Relationship	Occasion	Month Due	Gift	Payment Method	Budgeted Cost	Actual Cost	Variance

CHRISTMAS EXPENSE WORKSHEET

Overview

Christmas is traditionally the most expensive time of the year. Not alone are you likely to purchase gifts for family members and friends, but you are also likely to incur a significant amount of expense buying other festive items such as Christmas trees, lights, decorations, cards, and so on. In addition to all this, you will also need to take account of any additional food costs, travel costs and even entertainment costs that you might have over the festive season. All of these expenses add up and, without careful planning and monitoring, can have a very adverse affect on your financial situation. This Christmas Expense Worksheet has been designed to help you plan where your money will go over the course of the holiday season. It will allow you to budget specific amounts to spend on gifts, festive items, food and entertainment, amongst other things and to track your spending when it occurs.

The Worksheet

The worksheet is divided up in to four specific sections namely gifts, decorations, holiday food & drink and miscellaneous. In the gift section, you can name the specific people that you wish to make gifts for and allocate a budget for each person. In the other three sections, you will be able to allocate specific budget amounts for each of the most common items that you will spend money on during the holiday season.

How to Complete this Worksheet

Having printed off the worksheet or saved a version to your computer, the first thing you may wish to do is set an overall budget amount for spending during the Christmas period. If so, this amount will be set out right at the top of the worksheet. If you are not sure what this figure is likely to be, you could wait until you have filled in the remainder of the worksheet in draft format before entering the overall budget amount.

The next step will be to go through each of the expense items listed in the first column (including the gifts) and allocate a budget amount for each of them. If there are any specific expenses not listed, you can list them yourself in the 'Miscellaneous' section. Remember to be as realistic and honest as possible in allocating your budget. There is no point including an amount of $10 for a Christmas tree when you know it will be at least $50 or more.

After you have included a budgeted amount for each item (or group of items) of expenditure, the next step will be to insert the actual cost of each item when you purchase it and then determine the difference between the budgeted cost and actual cost. This cost will be known as the 'variance'. As you make your purchases, some items will cost more than your budgeted amount and some will cost less. As a result, you should try to adjust the amount budgeted for other items as appropriate so that you can stay within your overall budget.

CHRISTMAS EXPENSE WORKSHEET

Budget Amount: _____

Gifts	Gift Details	Budget	Actual	Variance		
1						
2						
3						
4						
5						
6						
7						
Christmas Decorations						
Christmas Tree					**Budget Amount**	_____
Christmas Lights						
Christmas Ornaments					**Total Actual Spending**	
Wrapping Supplies					Christmas Decorations	_____
Christmas Cards					Holiday Food & Drink	_____
					Miscelleaneous	_____
Holiday Food & Drink						
Dining Out					**Total Varience**	_____
Food						
Party Food						
Cooking / Baking						
Beverages / Alcohol						
Miscelleaneous						
Clothing						
Charity / Donations						
Packaging / Postage						
Photographer						
Events / Parties						
Travel						
Entertainment						
Other Supplies						
Other Expenses						

VEHICLE BUDGET WORKSHEET

Overview

Apart from buying a home, vehicles are often the most expensive items that the average person will purchase. In addition to having large up-front costs, vehicles also have significant annual running costs. All of these factors need to be taken into account before deciding on a specific vehicle to buy. For this reason, it's a good idea to prepare a budget before you buy a vehicle. Not alone will a budget help you avoid over-spending but it will also allow you to easily compare the costs of two or more vehicles that you are thinking of purchasing. By entering a few details into the budget worksheet, you will get a clear picture of the total cost of purchasing your vehicle and more importantly whether you can afford it.

The Worksheet

The worksheet is divided up in to three specific sections namely vehicle information, income and expenses. In the vehicle information section, you can set out details of the vehicle you wish to purchase such as the make, model and year. In the income section, you can set out details of any income that you may generate using your new vehicle. This income may come in the form of payments based on miles travelled (millage) or a subsidy/allowance received from your employer. The expenses section includes some of the most typical types of expense associated with owning a vehicle. Of course, there may be others. If you need to fit out your vehicle in some way such as adding a hitch or fitting special lights or other additions, these will also need to be taken into account – both the cost of the fitting and the service fee for adding the fitting.

How to Complete this Worksheet

After you have printed a copy of the worksheet or saved it to your computer, start by adding the general information about the vehicle you are buying – make, model, etc. The next step will be to calculate whether you will make any income specifically from the vehicle itself. When you have done this, go through each of the expense items listed in the first column and allocate a budget amount for each of them. To do this, you will need to consider the approximate number of miles you will be driving each month and the miles per gallon (MPG) that you will obtain from your vehicle. The seller of the vehicle should be able to tell you precisely how many MPG the vehicle does. If not, you can look it up on the internet using sites such as http://www.fueleconomy.gov/. If you have borrowed to purchase your vehicle, your lease company or lending company should be able to confirm the precise monthly repayments that you will need to make. To obtain appropriate details for your insurance premiums, you could either contract your broker or ring around for a few quotes. For other items of expenditure such as the cost of servicing and repairs, you can either estimate them, find out what the vendor paid for such services (if it's a second hand vehicle) or ask your garage to give you a ball park estimate of the average service costs for similar vehicles. This should help you collect the final pieces of information that you require to complete the worksheet.

VEHICLE BUDGET WORKSHEET

Make of Vehicle _____   Mileage Rate _____

Model of Vehicle _____   Subsidence _____

Year of Vehicle _____

Income	Jan	Feb	Mar	Apr	May	Jun	Jul	Aug	Sep	Oct	Nov	Dec	Total
Mileage													
Subsidence													
Other													
Total Income													
Expenditure													
Fuel & Oil													
Maintenance & Repairs													
Tires													
Insurance													
License/ Registration													
Loan/Lease Payments													
Loan/Lease Interest													
Parking/ Storage													
Tolls													
Miscellaneous Expense s													
Total Expenditure													
Net Income													

WEDDING BUDGET WORKSHEET

Overview

Weddings, as we all know, can be expensive. However, they can be even more expensive if you fail to properly budget for the big day. In many cases, people planning weddings tend to focus on the larger expenses (such as the cost of the venue, food, music, etc) to the detriment of smaller expenses (such as photos, invitations, etc). In doing so, they often inadvertently cause the costs of the wedding to increase significantly. For this reason, before making any plans or any bookings you need to carefully assess the likely costs of the wedding as a whole and budget accordingly. The attached Wedding Budget Worksheet helps you categorize wedding expenses while at the same time comparing budgeted costs to actual costs. When used correctly, it can be an exceptionally useful budgeting tool.

The Worksheet

This worksheet is divided into a number of different categories. Each category relates to a particular class of expense that you are likely to encounter when planning a wedding. For example, the expense classes include items such as reception costs, honeymoon costs, decoration costs and many more. Within each expense class, there is a list of the most commonly incurred expenses in that class. By having a list of all of these expenses to hand, it should ensure that you are less likely to forget some of the expenses involved. That said, there will of course be other expenses that you may wish to include that are not listed on the worksheet and you will need to include these as necessary yourself. Finally, there are two columns opposite each expense – "budget" and "actual". As the names suggest, one column is for the amount that you have budgeted for a particular expense, the other is for the actual cost of that expense.

How to Complete this Worksheet

Completing the worksheet is relatively straightforward, simply go through each of the expenses listed and insert an appropriate amount for your estimate of the likely cost of that expense. This will help you get an overall picture of the total cost of the wedding right from the outset. Then, as you agree terms with various service and goods providers, you can insert the actual amount of the expense into the relevant column. If you spend more or less on a particular item, you may wish to reduce or increase the amount allocated to other expenses so that your overall budget amount remains broadly in line with your original estimate.

Once you have completed all the various sections, transfer the totals from each section to the final table in the worksheet. This will then enable you to have a full review of your expenses as from your "budget" perspective and the "actual" outcome.

WEDDING BUDGET WORKSHEET

Clothing & Apparel

	Budget	Actual		Budget	Actual		Budget	Actual
Groom's Tuxedos			Jewelry & Accessories			Wedding Rings		
Groom's Shoes			Garter/ Stockings/ Hosiery			Bridal Gown		
Groomsmen's Tuxedos			Bridesmaids' Dresses			Veil/ Headpiece		
Groomsmen's Shoes			Bridesmaids' Accessories			Bridal Shoes		
Bridal Gloves			Bridesmaids' Shoes			Additional Expenses		

Total Budget: _____

Total Actual: _____

Flowers & Decorations

	Budget	Actual		Budget	Actual		Budget	Actual
Bride's Bouquet			Cermony Decoratinos			Balloons		
Bridesmaids' Bouquets			Reception Decorations			Transport Decorations		
Corsages			Candles & Lighting			Table Centerpieces		
Boutinere			Home Decorations			Additional Expenses		
Cermony Flower Arrangements			Reception Flower Arrangements					

Total Budget: _____

Total Actual: _____

WEDDING BUDGET WORKSHEET

Reception

	Budget	Actual		Budget	Actual		Budget	Actual
Location Fees			Drinks			Linens		
Tables & Chairs			Wedding Cake			Caterer		
Decorations			Staff Expenses			Gratuities		
Food			Reception			Music		

Total Budget: _____

Total Actual: _____

Stationary / Printing

	Budget	Actual		Budget	Actual		Budget	Actual
Cermony Invitations			Announcements			Seating/ Reception Cards		
Calligraphy			Cermony Booklets			Thank You Cards		
Response Cards			Guestbook			Postage / Stamps		

Total Budget: _____

Total Actual: _____

Honeymoon

	Budget	Actual		Budget	Actual		Budget	Actual
Air Tickets			Entertainment			Additional Expenses		
Car Rental			Visa					
Accomodation			Insurance					

Total Budget: _____

Total Actual: _____

WEDDING BUDGET WORKSHEET

Video & Photography

	Budget	Actual		Budget	Actual		Budget	Actual
Engagement Portraits			Photo Albums			Extras		
Cermony/ Reception			Videography					

Total Budget: _____

Total Actual: _____

Gifts

	Budget	Actual		Budget	Actual		Budget	Actual
Attendants' Gifts			Parents' Gifts			Groom's Party Gifts		
Bride and Groom Gift			Bridal Party Gifts					

Total Budget: _____

Total Actual: _____

Miscelleaneous

	Budget	Actual		Budget	Actual		Budget	Actual
Clergy / Officiant			Brunch			Additional Grooming Expenses		
Church/Ceremony Site Fee			Pre Wedding Parties			Rehersal Party		
Additional Ceremony fees			Marriage License			Limousine/ Carriage		
Rehersal Dinner			Transportation			Hairdresser		
Wedding Coordinator			Manicure/ Pedicure			Musicians for Cermony		
Hotel Rooms			Make-up					

Total Budget: _____

Total Actual: _____

WEDDING BUDGET WORKSHEET

Totals

	Budget	Actual
Video & Photography		
Clothing & Apparel		
Decorations		
Flowers & Decorations		
Gifts		
Honeymoon		
Miscelleaneous		
Music & Entertainment		
Reception		
Stationary / Printing		
Total		

WINDFALL PLANNER

Overview

Whether it's an inheritance, a bonus, or even a lottery win, it's always nice to receive a windfall of cash. However, as nice as it is to receive the money, it's more important that you put it to good use rather than wasting it. It may surprise you to learn that 1 out of every 3 lottery winners end up in financial trouble within 5 years of their big win. It happens because, having received a cash windfall, they foolishly rush out and blow their money through the purchase of non-essential items. To avoid a similar fate, it's always sensible to have a plan in place to cover the situation where you unexpectedly receive a large amount of cash. By having such a plan, you'll reduce the temptation to run out and book a holiday or buy a new car and will be more likely to repay your existing debts and your mortgage – something that will continue to benefit you long after your week long holiday would!

The Windfall Planner Worksheet is very straight forward. It allows you to set out how much you will receive and to then allocate that money between debt repayments, expense payments, savings, education and other goals. In deciding how to allocate your money, you should review some of your other budget worksheets to see what your expenses are, which debts need to be paid first, what goals you have, etc. Take your time and carefully consider what should be paid and in what order.

The Worksheet

The top of the worksheet contains a space to insert the amount of the windfall you expect to receive. The lower part of the worksheet is divided into three different columns – one for detailing the current amounts you owe or have put aside, one for detailing how much of the overall windfall amount you will use to pay off your debts or add to your savings and, finally, a column setting out the balance of your debts/savings after applying the windfall amount.

How to Complete this Worksheet

In order to complete the worksheet, the first thing that you will need to do is calculate the tax free amount of the windfall that you will receive. Remember, you will need to pay tax on bonuses and, in some cases, inheritances. Once you have done this, the next step will be to gather up your current financial statements so that you can then insert appropriate amounts for your current expenses, savings and desired spending (i.e. on goals, education, etc). Having done this, you will then need to allocate a specific amount from the windfall amount to be added to your savings, paid off your debts, etc. Remember, you don't have to spend the entire windfall amount - you can save some! Lastly, calculate the balance of your expenses and savings after applying the windfall amount. Seeing these balances will help motivate you towards applying the windfall amount to your savings and debts in the manner set out in your plan.

WINDFALL PLANNER WORKSHEET

Amount of Windfall: _____
Taxation on Windfall: _____
Net Available: _____

Expenditure	Amount Due	Drawings from Windfall	Windfall Balance
Mortgate Repayments			
Credit Card Repayments			
Loans Repayments			
Savings			
Retirement			
Investment			
Education			
Travelling			
Gifts			
Charities			
Other			
Total Expenditure			

MEDICAL EXPENSE WORKSHEET

Overview

Keeping track of your medical expenses can be particularly important especially if those expenses are in any way reimbursable through either medical insurance or tax deductions. This worksheet is specifically designed to help you track routine medical costs such as doctor, dentist and physiotherapy costs as well as the costs of more non-routine treatments such as chiropractor, acupuncture and similar treatments. In addition, if you have to pay for medical prescriptions, eye tests, glasses and other related medical expenses you can also take account of these in the worksheet.

The Worksheet

The worksheet is divided into a number of specific columns which allow you to enter specific information in relation to each medical treatment and cost including:

- the date of the medical cost;

- the name of the patient for whom the costs were incurred (which can be important if you have family health insurance);

- details of the healthcare provider – such as whether it's a doctor, physiotherapist, etc and the name and address of that provider;

- expense details such as whether the expense related to a visit to the doctor, a prescription, or other similar cost;

- the amount of the expense incurred; and

- details of the miles you travelled to obtain the medical treatment (which may be tax deductable).

How to Complete this Worksheet

Completing this worksheet is fairly straightforward. Simply print off a copy of the worksheet and add details of the medical expenses that you incur from time to time. For the purposes of claiming reimbursements of medical expenses (whether from a medical insurance policy or by means of a tax deduction) it's a good idea to attach all of your medical receipts to the back of the worksheet or at the least keep them together somewhere safe. This will make it a lot easier when the time comes for claiming these expenses.

MEDICAL EXPENSE WORKSHEET

Date	Patient Name	Healthcare Provider	Expense Details	Amount	Mileage

MEDICAL INSURANCE REIMBURSEMENT WORKSHEET

Overview

One of the main reasons for keeping track of your medical expenses is to ensure that you are in a position to claim them back from your insurance company when the time comes. This worksheet supplements the Medical Expenses Worksheet by helping you keep track of any medical expense claims that you have made against your health insurance.

The Worksheet

The worksheet is divided into a number of specific columns which allow you to enter specific information in relation to each claim including:

- the date the claim was submitted to the insurance company;

- details of the costs that you have claimed back (such as physiotherapy costs);

- the amount of the insurance reimbursement that you expect to receive;

- the amount of the insurance reimbursement that you have received;

- the amount of the insurance reimbursement that remains outstanding; and

- any general comments that you may have about the claim.

How to Complete this Worksheet

Completing this worksheet is relatively easy. Just print off a copy of the worksheet and add details of the claims that you make from time to time. The details can normally be taken directly from your insurance claim form. When making a claim it's often wise to retain a copy of the claim form you submit as well as a copy of all medical receipts submitted with the claim form just in case you need them in the future (for example, for claiming tax deductions).

MEDICAL INSURANCE REIMBURSEMENT WORKSHEET

Date of Claim	Claim Details	Expected Reimbursment	Actual Reimbursment	Reimbursment Outstanding	Comments

SUBSCRIPTION RECORD WORKSHEET

Overview

Many of us pay subscriptions for things such as magazines, sporting club memberships and organisational memberships. In most instances, the related subscription payments will need to be made either monthly, quarterly or annually. More often than not, these payments will be made directly from your bank account without you needing to do a thing. However, while you are relieved of the burden of arranging the payment each period, you will still need to keep a close watch on what you have paid for, the amount you have paid and the subscription period covered. This Subscription Record worksheet allows you to easily keep track of all of your subscription payments thereby ensuring that you get what you paid for and that you don't end up duplicating payments!

The Worksheet

The worksheet is divided into a number of columns and rows which allow you to enter specific details in respect of each subscription you make; details such as when the subscription was paid, the cost of the subscription, the amount paid, the payment reference number, etc. Having all of these details at your fingertips should make it a lot easier to manage and keep track of your subscriptions generally.

How to Complete this Worksheet

Completing the worksheet is easy. Just enter the name of the subscription in the left column and move across each column entering the required information. That's it!

SUBSCRIPTION RECORD WORKSHEET

Subscription Payee	Subscription Details	Amount Paid	Date of Payment	Payment Reference	Method of Payment	Exipiration/ Renewal Date	Auto Renewal	Subscription Duration

CHILD SUPPORT PAYMENT RECORDS

Overview

If you are a single parent or a custodial parent following a separation or a divorce, the receipt of child support payments can be of significant importance when it comes to you being able to meet the day to day living expenses of your children. As such, it's important to be able to track the monies that you receive from time to time in a sensible manner and to have a clear indication of how much you will be receiving and when. This worksheet will help you do just that. Similarly, if you are a non-custodial parent, you may also want to keep track of the monies that you pay out, to whom and when. This is because, apart from ensuring that your children will have sufficient funds available to them (albeit indirectly) you may also need to keep track of the payments where they form part of a divorce/ separation settlement agreement or have otherwise been ordered by a court. This worksheet will help you keep the necessary records to help demonstrate your compliance with such agreements and orders from time to time.

The Worksheet

The worksheet, which is child specific, is divided into a number of rows and columns. Each row represents a particular month of the year (as most payments are made monthly). In turn, each column contains space for details of the relevant payment such as the amount to be paid, the date of payment, details of where the payment is to be made, etc. You should complete one worksheet for each of your relevant children.

The columns in the worksheet are divided as follows:

- "Amount Due" – the amount due in a given month;

- "Amount Paid" – the amount paid in a given month;

- "Amount Outstanding" – the amount that remains owing in a given month;

- "Payment Date" – the specific date upon which a payment must be made in a given month;

- "Payment Method" – the means by which a monthly payment will be made such as by bank transfer, check, standing order, cash, etc. If you pay in cash, obtain a signed receipt.

- "Bank Account" – details of the bank account into which the payment should be made.

- "Additional Details" – any other relevant payment in relation to the particular monthly payment.

How to Complete this Worksheet

To complete this form, start by printing off a copy or saving a copy to your computer. Once you have done this, all you need to is enter the monthly payment details as required. For example, you will need to enter details of the amount paid, the date paid, the method of payment, etc.

CHILD SUPPORT PAYMENT RECORDS

Name of Child(s) _____   Current Balance Outstanding _____

_____

_____

	Amount Due	Amount Paid	Amount Outstanding	Payment Date	Payment Method	Bank Account	Additional Details
Jan							
Feb							
Mar							
Apr							
May							
Jun							
Jul							
Aug							
Sep							
Oct							
Nov							
Dec							

NET WORTH STATEMENT

Overview

One of the best ways to track your overall budgeting progress is to prepare a net worth statement. A net worth statement is a snapshot of your current financial position. It compares your total assets to your total liabilities and calculates the value of your assets after subtracting the total cost of all of your liabilities. If there is a positive balance remaining, this represents your 'net worth'. If your liabilities are greater than your assets then, unfortunately, you will have no net worth. Your overall goal will of course be to have a positive net worth and, after achieving that, to increase it each year.

The Worksheet

The worksheet is divided out in to two principal sections. The first section contains details of all of your assets such as cash, investments, savings, land, etc. The second section contains details of all of your liabilities such as mortgages, loans, credit card debts, etc. Your total assets, total liabilities and net worth (if any) are set out at the bottom of the form.

How to Complete this Worksheet

To complete the form, you will need to gather together details of all of your assets and liabilities. In the case of assets such as investments and real estate, you will need to get the most recent valuations reports for such assets. If you believe that the valuations set out in any of those reports have changed, you should insert what you believe to be the current fair market value of the asset. Your liabilities should be clearly identifiable from invoices and other statements. Once you have gathered together all of the relevant information, you should insert all of the relevant data into the worksheet and add up your total assets and liabilities. Once this is done, subtract the total asset figure from the total liability figure. If this gives you a positive figure, it will represent your net worth. If the figure is negative, it simply shows that you owe more than you own – which is not a healthy financial position to be in.

Net Worth Statement

Assets

	You	Spouse	Total
Cash/Bank			
Cash on Hand			
Bank - Checking Account			
Bank - Saving Account			
Cash Value of Life Insurance			
Credit Union			
Certificate of Deposits			
Other			
Investments			
Annuities			
Bonds			
Other			
Life Insurance			
Money Market Funds			
Mutual Funds			
Pension			
Stock			
Other			
Retirement Savings			
Pension			
401k or 403(b) Account			
IRA, RSPs, Superannuation Accounts			
Keogh Account			
Other			
Land/Property			
Real Estate			
Land			
Other			
Personal Property			
Automobile			
Additional/ Recreational Vehicles			

NET WORTH STATEMENT

Home Furniture			
Appliances & Equipment			
Jewelry			
Other			
Total Assets			
Liabilities			
Mortgage			
Primary Residence			
Home Equity Loan 1			
Home Equity Loan 2			
Other			
Loans			
Student Loan			
Automobile Loan			
Personal			
Other			
Other Liabilities			
Credit Card 1			
Credit Card 2			
Installment Plan			
Leases			
Other			
Expenses Overdue			
Household			
Bills & Utilities			
Transportation			
Family			
Healthcare			
Entertainment			
Total Liabilities			
Total Net Worth			

Retirement Planning Worksheet

Overview

Retirement can be a daunting experience for many people. Often you can become blindsided by the fact you no longer take home a pay check at the end of each week. Wondering how your daily needs are going to be fulfilled can cause substantial stress. Many retirees find that essential expenses can take up a large part of their income. Creating a budget to understand your income and expenditure is a smart decision and will help you avoid one of the most common pitfalls of retirement, spending to much to soon. Smart budgeting will enable you to spend retirement doing the things you like more, such as travel, engaging in activities or simply completing a home project.

The Worksheet

The worksheet is divided out in to two principal sections. The first section contains details of all of your income such as salary, pensions, investments, social security, etc. The second section contains details of all of your expenses such as household, bills & utilities, food & dining, etc. Your total income, total expenditure and net worth (if any) are set out at the bottom of the form.

How to Complete this Worksheet

To complete the form, you will need to gather together details of all of your incomes and expenditure for a given month. Enter the details of your monthly sources of income in the spaces provided. When finished, calculate your total income per month. Next, move to the expenditure section, you will now need to estimate the amount you wish to spend for each of the expense categories. If you are finding it difficult to identify your monthly spending in each category, we suggest you use the Monthly Expense Tracking Worksheet on Pg 103 to gain an understanding of your current spending. This will help you better understand and plan your retirement. Now that you have clearly identified your income and expenditure, subtract the total income figure from the total expenditure figure. If this gives you a positive figure, it will represent a positive retirement budget. If the figure is negative, it simply shows that you are spending more money than you taking in – which is not a healthy financial position to be in. In this case, it may be worthwhile to rethink your proposed retirement spending.

RETIREMENT PLANNING WORKSHEET

Monthly Income

Sources of Income	Amount
Salary 1	
Salary 2	
Pension	
Social Security	
Annuities	
IRA / 401K Accounts	
Investments	
Other Income	
Other Income	
Total Income	

Monthly Expenditure

Sources of Expenditure	Amount	Sources of Expenditure	Amount
Household		**Transportation**	
Home Repairs		Car Loan Repayment	
Household Goods		Car Repairs	
Mortgage Payments		Gas/Fuel	
Rent Payments		Parking/Tolls	
Other		Public Transport	
		Registration	
Bills & Utilities			
Cell Phone		**Family**	
Electricity		Activities	
Garbage		Child Care	
Heating		Child Support	
Internet		Clothing	
Cable / TV		Pet Expenses	
Water		School Expenses	
Other		Pocket Money	
Food & Dining		**Healthcare**	
Breakfast		Dentist	
Dinner		Doctor	
Groceries		Eye care	
Lunch		Medication	
Take Away		Rehabilitation	
Tea/Coffee/Snacks			

RETIREMENT PLANNING WORKSHEET

Sources of Expenditure	Amount	Sources of Expenditure	Amount
Miscellaneous		**Entertainment**	
Clothing		Books & Magazines	
Donations		Events	
Grooming		Movies & Theatre	
Investments		Music	
Loan		Travel	
Laundry/Cleaning			
Bank Charges			
Savings			
Gifts			
Other			
Other			
Total Expenditure			
Total Net Income			

INDEX

Other Great Books from Enodare's
Estate Planning Series

2nd Edition

enodare

Make Your Own

Living Trust
& Avoid Probate

- Avoid the delays and costs of probate
- Manage your assets during incapacity
- Leave money and property to your loved ones
- Save money and reduce taxes

Living Trust Forms Included!

Estate Planning Series

Enodare is a renowned worldwide leader

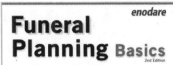

enodare

Estate
Planning Essentials
3rd Edition

Learn How To:
- Prepare an effective estate plan
- Provide for children and other beneficiaries
- Plan for medical incapacity
- Save on legal fees & taxes
- & much more......

Estate Planning Worksheets Included!

Estate Planning Series

Enodare is a renowned worldwide leader

enodare

Funeral
Planning Basics
2nd Edition

A Step-By-Step Guide to Funeral Planning

- Arrange your funeral service
- Decide on your final resting place
- Save on funeral costs and expenses
- Save your family the burden of funeral planning

Includes Funeral Planning Worksheets

Estate Planning Series

Enodare is a renowned worldwide leader in do-it-yourself estate planning publications

---

3rd Edition

enodare

Make Your Own

Last Will
& Testament

- Leave money and property to your loved ones
- Avoid intestacy
- Appoint guardians for your children
- Save on legal and probate fees

Create A Will & Protect Your Family!

Estate Planning Series

Enodare is a renowned worldwide leader

enodare

2nd Edition

How to Probate
an Estate

A Step-By-Step Guide for Executors

- Initiate and close probate with ease
- Learn how to locate and manage estate assets
- Deal with creditors' claims, taxes and trusts
- Avoid the common mistakes made by many executors

Sample Probate Forms Included!

Estate Planning Series

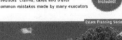

Enodare is a renowned worldwide leader

3rd Edition

enodare

Make Your Own

Medical & Financial
Powers of Attorney

- Appoint someone to mange your financial affairs
- Have someone make medical decisions for you
- Ensure that your family is not left helpless
- Avoid a depletion in the value of your assets

Power of Attorney Forms Included!

Estate Planning Series

Enodare is a renowned worldwide leader in do-it-yourself estate planning publications

---

2nd Edition

enodare

Make Your Own

Living Will

Everything You Need To Prepare Your Own Living Will!

- Specify your preferences for end-of-life treatments
- Avoid unwanted medical procedures
- Avoid family disputes
- Reduce healthcare costs

All 50 State Forms Included!

Estate Planning Series

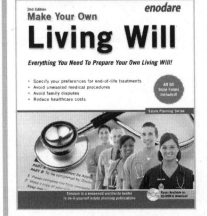

Enodare is a renowned worldwide leader in do-it-yourself estate planning publications

Wills Made Easy

Estate Planning Series

Legal Will Kit

All the ready-to-use lawyer approved forms, worksheets and step-by-step instructions you need to prepare your own personalised Last Will & Testament.

✓ Leave Money & Gifts to Your Family and Friends
✓ Appoint Guardians for Your Children
✓ Make Huge Savings on Legal Fees

Includes 2011 Legal & Tax Updates!

enodare

Enodare in a renowned worldwide leader in do-it-yourself estate planning publications

Trusts Made Easy

Estate Planning Series

Living Trust Kit

All the ready-to-use lawyer approved forms, worksheets and step-by-step instructions you need to prepare your own personalised living trust.

✓ Avoid the Substantial Costs & Delays of Probate
✓ Leave Money & Gifts to Your Family and Friends
✓ Make Huge Savings on Legal Fees

Includes Living Trust Forms!

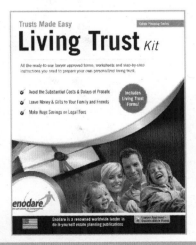

enodare

Enodare is a renowned worldwide leader in do-it-yourself estate planning publications

---

www.enodare.com

Entrepreneur's Guide to Starting a Business

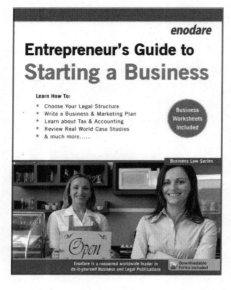

Entrepreneur's Guide to Starting a Business takes the fear of the unknown out of starting your new business and provides a treasure chest of information that will help you be successful from the very start. First-time entrepreneurs face a daunting challenge in identifying all of the issues that must be addressed and mastered when starting a new business. If any item slips through the cracks, or is handled improperly, it could bring a new company crashing to the ground. Entrepreneur's Guide to Starting a Business helps you meet that challenge by walking you through all of the important aspects of successfully launching your own business.

When you finish reading this book, not alone will you know the step-by-step process needed to turn your business idea and vision into a successful reality, but you'll also have a wealth of practical knowledge about corporate structures, business & marketing plans, e-commerce, hiring staff & external advisors, finding commercial property, sales & marketing, legal & financial matters, tax and much more.

Features:

- Comprehensive overview of all major aspects of starting a new business

- Covers every stage of the process, from writing your business plan to marketing and selling your new product

- Plain English descriptions of complex subject matters

- Real-world case study showing you how things play out in an actual new business environment

www.enodare.com